HOW TO MANAGE YOUR BOSS

And Get Them To Act Like
A Reasonable Human Being

Reduce Stress…

Create Harmony…

Bring About Calm At Work…

In 4 Easy Stages

MARK LEWIS

IN FOND REMEMBRANCE OF

Beverley Stainthorpe Lewis

My Sister

And

Sarah

My Cullercoats Girl

Published in Great Britain 2019
by Mark Lewis

Reprinted 2020

A CIP catalogue record for this book is available
from the British Library.

ISBN: 978-1-0709001-3-1

Book cover designed by
Ross Baker at Urban Media UK

Book design by chandlerbookdesign.com

Printed in Great Britain by
Kindle Direct Publishing

CONTENTS

About the Author   1

About the Author – The Back Story   3

About this Brilliant Little Book   6

1. What Is Managing Up?   8

2. A Little Bit About the Different Types of Boss …   13
   The Different Levels of 'Difficult'

3. Understanding that Difficult Bosses Can Hurt!   17

4. The 'Six Scenario' Analysis (Is It Me?'):   25

5. It's Time for a Change – It's Time for Action!   39

6. Understanding Your Boss: 43

7. 'Let's Talk'… Having 'That' Conversation with   50
   Your Boss

8. The Full Conversation – The 4 Key Steps   99

9. A Few Final Thoughts (A Few Final Doubts?)   110

BONUS CHAPTER 1
Something for the Bosses: 115

BONUS CHAPTER 2
Managing Up…& The Boss Who Is Not Too Bad   119

BONUS CHAPTER 3
General Tips to Help the Workplace Relationship   123

About the Author

Mark Lewis is the co-founder and CEO of The Brilliant Training Company Limited, a Berkshire based company that specialises in communication-based training. Mark has extensive international business experience in sales, marketing and management.

Embarking on a career in fashion retailing, he was managing his own store in the UK and controlling a staff of 15 by the age of 21. By the age of 24 he had progressed his career and joined a major UK PLC fashion retailer as a Regional Manager, controlling 15 major stores with a total staff of 150.

Moving into Sales & Marketing, Mark was National Sales Manager for Europe's largest leisure company where he was responsible for recruiting, training and managing a national sales force of 40 sales managers. From there he progressed further to become Head of Sales & Marketing for one of Europe's most successful Airlines.

In 2006, Mark co – founded The Brilliant Training Company, an organisation of which he is CEO. A passionate human development specialist, he is also a highly experienced and sought-after public speaker.

Mark has appeared on radio and TV and both the UK and Europe and regularly delivers Brilliant Training to a range of companies as well as providing communication coaching and mentorship to senior board members of a number of leading UK PLCs.

Mark has a daughter and lives in Berkshire.

About the Author – The Back Story

Writing the previous biog I have to say it all sounds rather splendid and it does tend to make me seem a very clever boy – however, while every word is totally true there is, of course, the proverbial back story!

As a child I was painfully shy (chronically so) and so my early life tended to be full of things that terrified me, the main one being school. Apparently my first day at school I was so traumatised I spent the whole morning leant forward, arms folded on the desk, head on my arms, refusing to either look at anyone, talk to anyone or take my coat off.

As you will see from the formal account of my life, at times I have done ok and even quite well, but at school I was hopeless and being slightly dyslexic only added to the serious challenges I had with learning. I was pretty good at sport but really poor academically and I left school just before my seventeenth birthday with no formal qualifications at all (to this day I have neither a university degree, nor an A Level or an O Level to my name).

My first job was working in a warehouse in the village where I lived and I hated it. I stuck it for about a year and a half until one day I could stand it no more and literally just walked out, never to go back. From there, aged about 19, I was unemployed for a while until I finally got myself a job as a Saturday Boy working in a shop selling jeans... I loved it! After a couple of months, a full-time position became available and I was back in full time employment!

So that is how I got into selling and how I quite quickly got into managing people – as, within ten months of starting as a lowly sales assistant, I had been promoted through the ranks to become Manager of the company's Nottingham store. I had arrived, but unfortunately not for long!

I was Manager for about a year when I decided that I should be the next big entrepreneur, so I left and went into business (if you can call selling T shirts on the markets of the East Midlands 'in business') but I failed horribly. However, lady luck did indeed have me in her sights and somehow I managed to get back into retailing, but this time as an Area Manager for what was, at the time, one of Britain's leading fashion outlets. (To this day I'm still not sure how I landed what was a very big job, but I did!)

From there it's been a journey that has had some big successes – but equally one or two little setbacks too and it's never been the classic 'Smart guys inevitable rise to the top'. At school I was perhaps the one 'least likely to succeed' but what I discovered (though I didn't realise it at the time) was that everything is a learning experience and there is a positive to be had from just about every set back.

I have been made redundant three times, demoted once and even sacked once, but as you can see above, I have also held some pretty big jobs and had some considerable success too. In 2006, I co-founded The Brilliant Training Company and that's what I have been doing ever since.

We specialise in communication-based training – which in itself is pretty bizarre for a person who was so incredibly shy and who found communicating with just about anyone a terrifying experience.

However, perhaps it's the very fact that I know just how it feels NOT to be able to communicate that has given me the insights I now have (like I said, there is a benefit to all bad experiences if we care to look for it and acknowledge it).

So that's me! I'm most certainly not an intellectual who was bound for glory from day one, but more a very shy little boy who somehow 'found a way' to find a way, though like I said, it's had a few challenging moments.

So out of this background comes this Brilliant Little Book. I truly hope the ideas, suggestions and strategies contained in it help to bring a little calm to the relationship you have with your boss. I'm sure they will.

About this Brilliant Little Book

Rocket science is indeed a complex affair, as is quantum physics and surgery on the human brain!

In this busy world of ours it is true that many things can have the 'COMPLEX' warning stamped all over them – but in the area of 'Communication in business' & 'Communication in the work place', things are in effect quite simple – or they were until we muddied the waters and made it difficult for ourselves.

Unless we are fortunate enough to be born into great riches or we win the lottery, most of us have to work for a living, and for those who don't take time away from the workplace to bring up children there are about 48 years of the 9 till 5 stuff that we have to encounter. So, with so much 'time at work' to get through, it's perhaps understandable that occasionally we will encounter challenges, not just with the tasks we have to apply ourselves to (our work) but also the human interaction with the people we come into contact with – be it our colleagues or, of course, our boss!

It is true that sometimes when we look back on old relationship challenges, we can come to the conclusion that with hindsight it was really not too bad and we can't understand why it was so stressful and even upsetting to us. But at the time these niggly and often unpleasant situations seem very real indeed – and even worse, the solutions needed to bring calm to our lives can seem very hard to find.

Communication is at the heart of all human interaction and if we can get the communication right it can greatly improve the quality of our lives. However, communication is very complex – or is it?

Enter Brilliant Little Books

The concept of all of the books in the Brilliant Little Books range is to offer a straightforward and simple guide on such things as Managing People, Leadership, Presentation Skills, Being Happy and this one, Managing Your Boss.

The books are not be filled with hi-brow gobbledegook, nor are they on a quest to use the very latest business jargon. They will not give you a headache reading them and they will not leave you thinking 'Mmmm...interesting...but what the hell do I do now and how do I implement all of this?'.

Instead you get a clear and easy to read manual that will give you straightforward tips, techniques, attitudes and tools to improve your business performance, make you more effective, help you get on better with everyone and anyone and generally make your life easier. On top of this, each book in the Brilliant Little Book range is guaranteed to take less than ninety minutes to read, so reading it will not become a War & Peace test of endurance.

So welcome to Brilliant Little Books...

They are Brilliant...

They Are Little...

...And They Work!

1
What Is Managing Up?

Managing Up is a very simple process that will give you some very real skills, techniques, tools, tips and attitudes to enable you to manage your boss more effectively – and so develop a more harmonious and pleasant working relationship.

Managing Up can mean no more worrying, no more stress, no more sleepless nights, no more feeling undervalued, no more feeling humiliated, no more feeling ignored and definitely no more of those 'Shall I leave?' thoughts. It can also put an end to feelings of frustration and doubt, as well as stopping hurtful comments, sarcasm and even subtle bullying, blatant bullying and aggression.

Put simply, by adopting some of the simple & straightforward techniques in this Brilliant Little Book, even the most difficult relationship with the most onerous boss can be transformed.

This book is not a heavy intellectual read that will overwhelm you with highbrow terminology and pseudo psychology, but more a simple, highly effective manual that can take the relationship with your boss from difficult to delightful...painful to peaceful. Better still it will not take five hours to read and reading it will not give you a headache. It will, however, work!

It will assist you with a boss who's really pretty dreadful and makes your life hell – but it also contains strategies and tips that can be invaluable in helping along the relationship with a boss who, all in all, is not too bad, but perhaps could be better, the boss who has one or two bad habits that occasionally frustrate, annoy and hinder your effectiveness and your happiness at work.

It's applicable to the male boss, the female boss and the young boss, the old 'set in their ways' boss and the boss who you are certain was not actually born – but was created by the devil.

However, before we go any further, let's establish two very important points…

ONE:

This book is most definitely NOT anti- boss.

Now I know and accept that at time we may scratch our heads and wonder just what do these bosses actually do all day? In addition, we may also conclude that we ourselves could easily do their job infinitely better than they can. But in most instances, bosses have a very demanding job that more often than not includes more work, more pressure and a lot more stress than our own jobs.

So, while we may occasionally conclude that the world would be a better place without managers, line managers, supervisors, bosses, or whatever you want to call them – bosses are of course essential and in many cases they do a great job, often under very difficult circumstances.

So, bosses are not the devil incarnate and they are not bad. We need bosses… though perhaps it's true we also need them to be a little better at managing us!

TWO

This book is <u>not</u> aimed at the type of person whose daily objective is to do as little as possible at work while simultaneously expecting to have a fantastic relationship with their boss. This type of employee is, of course, out there – but it's fair to say that if they take this type of attitude into the work place then the chances of having the said great working relationship are greatly diminished.

So, this book is based on a few key understandings, namely that we appreciate it's not good to start each day with an apologetic *'Ohhh. Sorry I'm late again'* – and then make a leisurely coffee before going on an even more leisurely wander to catch up on the gossip with colleagues. It **is** however based on the understanding that it is right and fair to work hard and generally be a reasonable human being who is polite, helpful and cooperative and who, in brief, tries to deliver the proverbial fair day's work for a fair day's pay.

Now, of course, being the late 'coffee making wanderer' as described above is not a criminal offence and it's not a sin – but being that type of employee will make it hard for anyone to have a fair and harmonious relationship with the boss!

So Where Did this Book Come From?

Well its origins really came from my own experiences. Being of a certain age and never having worked for a company for more than five years you can see I have had quite a few bosses. Of these, one or two have been fantastic and wonderful, some have been fair and ok but regrettably some have been downright awful, to the point where I was certain that investigation into their family tree would have revealed ancestral links to Genghis Khan, Attila the Hun – or both!

So, from my own experience I know just what it feels like to suffer at the hands of an inconsiderate and unfeeling boss, someone who doesn't understand you and the challenges you are encountering and someone who doesn't seem to care to find out. In addition, I also know the agonies we can go through when we ask ourselves the questions *'Why can't I handle them?'* – or worse still *'Shall I leave?'*

In addition to my own personal experiences, I run a training organisation called The Brilliant Training Company, an organisation that specialises in communication skills training, and managing your boss is DEFINITELY about communication. As a result, I meet people from all different vocational backgrounds on the courses that we run.

Now, as you would expect, each course has an agenda, but on a good 90% of all the training we deliver some brave sole will find the courage to ask the question that nearly always gets asked, namely *'Is there anything on the course about dealing with a difficult boss?'*

Finally, in my work with Brilliant Training, I do a lot of one-to-one coaching and over the years it's true that at least 50% of the people I have helped have had a challenge that can loosely be summarised by the statement *'I can't work with my boss…I think I need to leave'*.

So, from this background comes this book, a book that will lead you through a very simple, tried and tested Four Step plan to adjust and realign the behaviour of your boss and bring harmony, mutual respect and calm to your working life.

But before we make a start on the journey, let's firstly ask, and then answer one important question, namely:

'Is it wrong to set out on a premeditated campaign to change my boss?'

Well, of course, the answer to that question has to be a resounding NO!

By reading this book you are not acting in an underhand way and you are not scheming, disloyal, sneaky or manipulative. The fact that you have invested in this book means that it's likely you have a real problem, a problem that needs to be addressed. However, chances are that by addressing your problem not only will <u>you</u> benefit from the positive changes in 'boss behaviour' – but ultimately, and as a result of the increased harmony, your boss and your organisation will too, and that has to be a good thing.

So, welcome to a small and special group of people, a group of people who are not willing to suffer anymore, a small group of people who will no longer take the frustration and the pain – but who will act. A group of people who, via the strategies contained in this book will bring about a change in their boss for the better – so that a peaceful, respectful and mutually beneficial relationship is built.

So, step forward, have some faith and make a change. Change your boss and 'Manage Up'...it really is VERY easy.

2

A Little Bit About the Different Types of Boss … The Different Levels of 'Difficult'

Unlike species from the animal kingdom, bosses have not, as such, been categorised, which in many ways is a shame as it would make things so much easier if each one came with a warning such as 'Beware…Venomous' or 'Take Care – Scratches & Bites'; but sadly they don't. However, one thing is for sure, just like the occupants of the animal kingdom they do come in all shapes and sizes and all manner of degrees of difficult – and with a working UK population of thirty-two million (and 155 million in the USA) there are a lot of them out there… and most of us have one!

So, this being the case, it's hard to cover all of the different types of line managers, supervisors, team leaders, managers, bosses or whatever title you want to call the person who generally holds the power.

It could well be the case that your particular boss is not too bad at all and it's only occasionally that he/she displays behaviour and traits that make your life frustrating or difficult. On the other hand, even in these more enlightened days, when anything that even resembles bullying in the workplace is quite rightly totally outlawed, you could suffer at the hands of a boss like this – even if their totally unacceptable behaviour is dispensed in a subtler form than in the bad days of old.

So, with these two ends of the scale in mind, we have the 'Difficult Chart' – an approximate guide to help you plot just where your particular boss sits.

The Difficult Chart:

Level Zero:	Your boss is essentially fine and you have a good working relationship. While they are the boss and they do, of course, manage you, you're very much ok with this. They are fair and reasonable and their management style gives you no problems at all.
Level 1 to 3:	By and large as above except for 'now and again' moments when, for example, they don't listen, they interrupt and so talk over you, they don't respect your ideas, they are inconsistent with what they want from you or they are unavailable etc. etc. They are never really aggressive with you, but more, on occasions, annoying.
Level 4 to 7:	At this level, things are generally not too great. They do all of the things in Level 1 to 3 but are also at times unfriendly, very unapproachable, overtly critical, micro-managing in their style, not trusting, inconsistent in their mood and not too pleasant to be around. They very rarely motivate or inspire you and a lot of the time you feel you are walking on egg shells with them.
Level 8 to 10:	All of the above, but in addition anything that resembles a good working relationship is pretty much non-existent. They can be harsh, hurtful and very critical and they cause you worry, anxiety and even stress. If they left you would be elated – and how they make you feel gives you cause to think you need to leave the company in order to escape them.

Now, of course, the Difficult Chart is not an official chart and it is not a formal way of grading your or anyone's boss. It is just a very simple tool to help us roughly identify where any boss sits on the dreadful to great scale.

Yours may only be a two or a three...generally fine, but still however challenging enough to make your life hard work and even unpleasant at times. By contrast, they may unfortunately be up in the high nines or even a ten and you truly do suffer badly.

The good news is that most bosses who even make it onto the Difficult Chart occupy the bottom end of the scale. They are, by and large, not bad individuals at all, but it is more the case that they are not too accomplished at dealing with the finer points of people management.

Also, interestingly it's only in very rare cases that a boss is aware they are at the top of the scale but simply does not care. Most who are in this category may indeed have an idea that they are difficult to work for, but ultimately, they have no idea just how unpleasant the experience really is and it's a rare individual who knowingly causes distress and upset but continues to do it anyway.

So, with all of this said, when in this book we focus on the 8 to 10 end of the scale and talk about difficult, challenging, horrible, onerous, demotivating, sarcastic, unhelpful, picky, rude or downright aggressive bosses...and yours by comparison is nothing like this, then please bear with me. Some people really do suffer at the hands of people who, quite frankly, should not hold the title of manager or boss.

So, whatever level of 'Difficult' your particular boss is, this book can and will definitely help you.

It's there to assist the person whose boss is really not too bad – but who does have a few unwelcome and unpleasant traits that you would love to talk to them about. At the other end of the scale, it is there to help the person who truly struggles with the boss from hell and whose life is made a misery.

Whatever the level of 'Difficult' there IS a solution.

KEY MESSAGES:

- Bosses come in all shapes and sizes and in various degrees of 'Difficult'

- Your particular boss may be quite low on the scale and really not too bad, but this does not mean the relationship can't be improved. This book can help you do that.

- Sadly, there are bosses out there who are downright dreadful to work for. If you are unfortunate to work for one of these people then bringing about a positive change is essential. This book will again show you how to do just that.

3

Understanding that Difficult Bosses Can Hurt!

Having invested in this book, there is a good chance that you already agree with the above statement, but as we start the journey to find the solution and the key to bringing about positive change, it is important to remember just how damaging and detrimental a difficult boss can be.

Here are just three alarming statistics…

> A Gallup poll of more than 1 million U.S. workers concluded that the No. 1 reason people quit their jobs is a bad boss or immediate supervisor.

> A survey by Harvard Business Review found that 58% of employees surveyed said they would trust a complete stranger more than their own boss.

> The same Gallup poll as above confirmed that 78% or people who leave a company don't dislike the company or the work they do – they leave to get away from their boss.

The above statements are certainly true; a difficult boss can make your working life and indeed your life in general very unpleasant – to the point where your actual wellbeing can start to seriously suffer.

They, of course, impact on your working life and your existence between the Monday to Friday working hours of 9 to 5 can turn out to be pretty miserable.

With this in mind, I often think how odd it is that when we attend an interview for a new job, we spend so little time examining and considering the relationship side of things with our potential future boss.

Of course, actual time with the boss varies from company to company and person to person but if we work in close proximity, say in an office environment, then it's possible that in any given week, we will on average spend about 30 hours in the vicinity or company of our boss, which by a quirky and ironic coincidence is about the same amount of quality waking hours the average person spends with their loved one, be it husband, wife or general partner of choice.

However, when choosing our partner is it not true that most of us take a good degree of time in the 'interview' process that is normally called courtship!

In courtship we date them, we introduce our friends to them (and then of course get the all-important friend feedback) and we introduce them to our parents. We socialise together, shop together and go away for weekends together and then, if all is still looking good, we take the big step of trying two weeks exclusively in their company with a holiday! Then, finally, if it's still green lights all around, it's the big commitment and we marry – or at least move in together.

All in all, this entire decision making and checking out process normally takes on average anything from six months to two years. So, you will see that we tend to take our time when choosing who will get our precious 30 hours a week!

Compare this with the amount of time and thought we spend when selecting the other person in our life who we will commit said 30 hours to – our boss!

Normally it's an hour's interview and sometimes, if you're lucky, a second interview of similar duration, during which time the average boss will, of course, tell you all manner of facts about how it's a caring company, how they believe in openness and fairness and that you will be joining a great team.

Based on this briefest of exchanges, you commit to the 'marriage' and then, a few weeks later you are sat there thinking *'Why did I ever take this job?...I seem to be working for the boss from hell'*. It's a scary but very real fact!

So, during the hours of 9 to 5, Monday to Friday, a bad boss can really hurt. However, the influence of the difficult boss, that person who at times seems to go out their way to cause you discomfort and pain can also impact on home life as well.

We know there are varying degrees of difficult bosses, but when they are truly challenging, they really can have a very negative impact on your entire life. The relationship with your partner can be affected, as can the relationship with your children, parents and friends. In addition, a challenging boss can affect our mood and our sensibility, to the point where watch out unsuspecting stranger who just happens to ask you for directions as you make your commute home after a particularly bad day. They are taking their life into their hands and will do well to survive your response!

So, sadly, but very commonly, a bad boss who you are not able to manage and influence accordingly can have an incredibly stressful and so negative impact on your life, and not just during the working hours!

When We Take the Boss Home!

You have had a terrible day at work and your ideas have been treated with contempt. Your suggestions have been ignored, your work is never good enough and all in all your confidence, self-esteem and belief in yourself as a professional have been pretty much drained. This being the case of course it's only natural that when you finally get home there is a big desire to rid yourself of the frustration and anger you feel by sharing, or 'off-loading' this with a loved one.

The result of this is that while it's the last thing you actually want or need you have, in effect, taken your boss home with you. OK, I admit you certainly didn't set a place at the dinner table for them but the reality is they might as well be sat there, dining with you and your family.

Now when you do confide in a loved one or a close friend, these precious people in our lives do try to understand and their advice and comments are, of course, well meaning. But is it not true that in reality they cannot and do not understand just how bad it is, nor do they appreciate just how bad your boss can make you feel?

Against this background, we tend to get one of two types of response from our loved ones or friends…

RESPONSE ONE:

Is a well-meaning, but ultimately worthless overdose of sympathy. Yes, this initially makes us feel a little better but as the effect wears off, we realise that it will do absolutely nothing at all to solve the problem. Then, after the sympathy, we normally get the advice which, though well intended, tends to be totally inappropriate and so not much use at all. (This is not really their fault as they just don't understand or appreciate the subtle intricacies of the discomfort and pain you have to endure.)

RESPONSE TWO

Response Two tends to be of even less help than Response One and it is just what you **don't** want to hear. Yes, of course, we understand that our partner, (or brother, sister, parent or friend) is sincerely trying to help when they decide to give you their little pep talk with statements like…

'You need to stand up for yourself… why do you let them talk to you that way?'

However, if we knew the answer to that question, and goodness knows we have asked it enough times of ourselves, then we wouldn't have invested in this book would we!

So, the end result is that sharing the pain may indeed help us feel a little better for a short period of time, but deep down it's perhaps true that sharing our troubles with our loved ones or close friends actually does little to resolve the problem, and indeed, bringing it home with us can cause fractiousness in the family unit.

So, on some nights, the onerous and unpleasant boss comes home with us, but for some it can be even worse and, if we are not careful, we discover that our weekends are also invaded by the boss from hell.

I speak from very personal experience when I say that if someone suffers with a particularly challenging boss, only they can know the feeling of sheer delight, euphoria and joy as 5pm on a Friday comes around and two days of unadulterated boss-free joy begins.

Friday night, no matter what we do is just total bliss. However, no sooner have we got to Saturday morning than the joy alarmingly starts to evaporate and our thoughts, slowly at first, start to drift towards Monday morning and that endless question *'What mood will they be in?'*

The BIG Conclusion

It's vitally important to understand that having an unreasonable boss, a boss who you struggle to manage, can really hurt. They can steal your confidence, your self-esteem and your self-belief and they can certainly be the cause of huge amounts of stress. In addition, they can make us medically ill and even shorten our life span!

Research at the Karolinska Institute in Stockholm studied almost 20,000 workers across various industries in Sweden, Finland, Germany, Poland and Italy. The study found that the longer someone has a poor manager, the higher the risk of them suffering a serious illness such as a heart attack in the next ten years. In a further study focusing on workers in Stockholm, they found that male residents of the city were 25% more likely to have heart problems up to ten years later if they were unhappy with their boss at the start.

In addition, a report by the British Safety Council informs us that in 2017/18 a staggering 15.4 million working days were lost to work-related stress, anxiety or depression. Further, 57% of all days lost to ill health were due to stress and anxiety.

So, having a challenge and a problem with your boss can be a serious matter.

They can make you short-tempered with loved ones at home and they can lead to more than the odd sleepless night. They can cause you to eat badly (either too much or not enough) and they can be the cause of an unhealthy reliance on alcohol.

They definitely make our time at work very unpleasant and stressful but they are also the unwanted invader at home, both in the week but often at weekends too. They can make us feel sad, upset, frustrated, downright unhappy and incredibly angry – and often with ourselves for not being able to deal with them how we would want to.

Now, when this particular phenomenon happens, it can really be very damaging as we battle to answer the questions that continually seems to swirl around our head, namely…

'Why do I allow them to talk to me like that?'
'Why don't I say something?'
'Why didn't I say X Y or Z to them?'

This situation is proven to be very toxic and it can really take us to a bad place.

We know we are being treated in a bad way and we know for sure that we have a right to speak up and say something…and that we <u>should</u> speak up and say something – but, of course, we are not sure how to do this so we hesitate, procrastinate and ultimately do nothing.

As a result, we find ourselves in a vicious circle where we experience frustration, anger and pain at the hand of our challenging boss but then also berate ourselves for not having the courage to speak to them about it. This double whammy can truly damage us – often more than we think.

So, it is important to understand and appreciate that the discomfort we experience at the hand of our boss IS very real.

Now this all sounds pretty gloomy, I admit, and having painted a depressing picture, a picture that might just strike a chord, you are probably thinking *'Yes, this is just how it is …but what can I do about it?'*

Well the good news is there IS a solution – and you have it in your hands right now. For no matter how bad the situation is, it CAN be changed, both radically, totally and beyond recognition.

In brief, the tips, the techniques the simple strategies and the plan contained in this book will enable you, no matter how apprehensive, to have the conversation that you have always dreamed of having – and yes it goes JUST as you want it to.

What this book sets out is a tried and tested method and approach that can and will bring peace and harmony to the most difficult and fractious of 'boss/employee' relationships.

Interested?...

        … Want to know more?

           …Want to enter a new world?

THEN READ ON!

KEY MESSAGES:

- A difficult and challenging boss can have a very negative impact on you and your relationship with family, loved ones and friends.

- Challenging bosses are ruining workplaces, causing mental health issues and stressing out employees.

- All of this is not some small annoyance that you should just live with. It is a very real and acknowledged problem in the workplace.

- There IS a solution.

4
The 'Six Scenario' Analysis (Is It Me?'):

So, we now understand that a difficult and challenging boss can really have a negative impact on us, but more importantly we are also starting to understand that we can actually do something about it and so bring about a real change.

So hopefully, having fired up some desire and belief that change can be brought about, the first stage of the journey to a more harmonious working life is to ask yourself a VERY important question…

Is It Me – Am I Partly the Cause?

Now at this point, I understand that you may well be thinking something like, *'Ok, I buy a book about Managing Up and changing my boss and almost straight away I'm asked if I'm a contributor to my boss's behaviour'* – but please let me explain.

Here is an imaginary story about you and your gardener Steve…

You are a successful person who lives in a nice house with a lovely big garden. However, while you like your garden, you don't actually enjoy gardening. In addition, though you work from home you are always very busy. The solution?…You employ a gardener one day a week.

Your gardener is called Steve and the agreement you come to is a payment of £80 for one full day of gardening from 9 till 5.

The first two visits by Steve go well. He is friendly and initially seems to do a good job. But fast forward six weeks and things have changed. You have noticed that Steve very rarely arrives by 9 and when he does get to your place, he seems in no hurry to make a start!

The breaks that he is entitled to take far longer than the agreed 15 minutes and Steve will often sit in his van reading the newspaper for more like 25 minutes. In addition, his one-hour lunch break follows a similar pattern and is always more like 80 minutes. He is constantly taking calls from his friends and he loves to have lengthy chats to your neighbours, should they be in their adjoining gardens.

On top of this, his standard of work has definitely slipped and it does not hit the agreed criteria. Grass cuttings are left everywhere, plants are not watered and often the garden is left looking untidy when he departs.

Over the period that you have observed this you have become exasperated with Steve and admittedly, at times, you have been a little short with him. You tried to improve the situation back in week four when you had a friendly chat to highlight that his standards where not really what was agreed. However, nothing much has changed.

Fundamentally, he is not doing things properly or as agreed. He is not keeping his side of the bargain, though he <u>does</u> of course still take his full wage of £80 at the end of his day with you!

Your exasperation and annoyance have grown and, rightly or wrongly, but perhaps understandably you have delivered the odd sarcastic comment and have not been too friendly or chatty. You have tried to be polite and civil to him but it's pretty hard, as fundamentally you feel Steve is taking advantage of you.

Things continue like this and it's now Steve's eighth week when, out of the blue, he asks if he can have a chat with you at lunchtime. At 1pm you duly go out into the garden to enquire what he wants to talk to you about. Steve looks you in the eye and says…

> *'I'm truly not trying to be difficult or challenging but recently some of your comments have been a little sarcastic and even harsh, and to be quite honest I think they have been unfair. I like looking after your garden but the way you have spoken to me has made me feel bad and I don't think I'm being treated as fairly as I should be.'*

QUESTION...

When Steve hits you with this statement, do you immediately have feelings of guilt about your behaviour towards him? Are you overcome with a huge desire to apologise? Do you desperately feel the need to atone for your behaviour? Do you want to hug Steve and tell him how sorry you are? Or are your thoughts more in line with the following…

> *'You cheeky devil – if you did what I pay you to do in the first place perhaps I wouldn't be in such a sarcastic mood!'*

The point behind the story is, of course, an obvious one

Common sense tells us that out of all the many thousands if not millions of people who suffer as a result of their boss's poor behaviour, some will, in effect, be contributors, if not the actual instigators of the situation. As was indicated in the introduction section, anyone who turns up late and delivers a poor standard of work while also generally displaying a poor attitude will, by definition, struggle to have a great relationship with their line manager, supervisor or boss.

Now again, anyone who falls into this category should not be classed as a work place sinner. In every workforce there will be a mixture of people. There will be the superstars, there will be the average good solid workers but there will also be the other type we have just described, the people who could do more and whose attitude could be better. The world is made up of all different types of people and the workplace is, of course, no different.

The real problem is that some of the people who fall into the 'Could Try Harder' 'Could Have a Better Attitude' or 'Could Do Better Work' categories are actually unaware that their performance <u>could</u> and perhaps <u>should</u> be better and in their eyes, their performance at work is just fine. As a result of this, when their boss picks them up on poor performance and speaks to them about it, they logically feel that the criticism is unjust.

However, the reality is that their boss is probably a fair and decent person. Their team member is falling well short of the acceptable standard of work and so they, the boss, feel understandable emotions of exasperation, frustration and even annoyance. The bottom line is that if the employee performed at a level that was fair and just then the boss would not need to act like he/she does.

So, the big message here is that not everyone who thinks they have a bad boss is right and, in some instances, it is the poor performance of the employee that evokes the unwelcome response from their boss.

However, if we move this scenario forward a little then the real danger is when the employee decides to have a conversation with their boss about what they perceive as their boss's unfair management of them. When this happens, the employee is very much in Steve the Gardener territory and they could easily find themselves in a position where their case for better treatment from their boss has been seriously undermined by their own less than perfect performance.

So as to truly highlight the importance of Step Two, let me ask you a question. Have you ever entered into an argument with someone only to discover half way through the argument that the facts you are basing your argument on are, in fact, a little shaky and your logic is questionable even to you?

Well, talking to your boss is exactly the same. To take action and talk to them about how the relationship might be improved for the good of all is a great thing but the conversation will not go how you intended if, half way through, your boss reels off a whole list of your misdemeanours, misdemeanours that lead you to conclude that they do indeed have a point!

Now, from my experience, in most cases where someone thinks they work for a difficult and challenging boss their assessment is spot on and they do, and so it is highly likely that despite turning in a great all round performance, you yourself are having to endure a range of poor and even bad treatment at the hands of a very real difficult boss (from here on in referred to as a DB). However, acknowledging that out of all the people who read this book there will be some, no matter how few, who could improve their situation by improving their own performance is a possibility we do need to consider.

So, all we are trying to do in this chapter is to simply step back and calmly and clinically measure the reality of the situation.

This involves you carrying out a simple Six Scenario analysis. Doing this will, firstly, give you the certainty that your complaints are very real and justified and that you are in the right but secondly, this certainty will also seriously boost your belief and inner confidence to move things forward in a positive way.

So, here's what I want you to do.

Completing the Six Scenario Assessment

Please take a large piece of paper and across the top, write the following four headings

DB Action	Just or / Unjust?	My Resulting Emotion	Their Communication

Then please follow the instructions contained in the three questions below...

ONE: DB ACTION

Under the heading 'DB ACTION' briefly describe the last six times your DB acted in a way that you felt was not right, not fair, unjust...or could just have been better. These might have been occasions where you felt you were unfairly criticised, ignored, ridiculed, not listened to, humiliated or talked over etc. You need to be honest in this process and not use selective memory.

TWO: MY RESULTING EMOTIONS

Under the heading 'MY RESULTING EMOTION' write down exactly the emotion that their action evoked in you.

THREE: THEIR COMMUNICATION

Regardless of whether you felt your DB's criticism was fair or not, under the heading 'THEIR COMMUNICATION', simply write 'Good' or 'Bad' to indicate if your boss communicated their displeasure in a professional and measured way, or if you felt the way they talked to you was unprofessional, sarcastic, harsh or overtly aggressive etc.

If you can't clearly recall six different occasions when you were unjustly treated then you might want to start afresh and identify them as the occur. However, a word of warning – making a detailed list of what you feel is your boss's poor behaviour is not a task to carry out during work time. Fairness in the workplace goes both ways and this is not what we are paid to do. In addition, we do not want to create a witch hunt environment where we are almost willing our DB to behave badly. As stated, fairness and honesty are vital.

So, one way or another, take a few moments to sit back and recall and log some information and evidence. To help the process along, your piece of paper might look a little like this...

DB Action	Just or / Unjust?	My Resulting Emotion	Their Communication
Criticised late work when a deadline was not established		Frustrated, undervalued & hurt	Good
Rudely interrupted me in a meeting		Embarrassed & humiliated	Bad
Said my sales results were appalling		De-motivated & destroyed	Bad
Mocked my idea in a meeting		Angry, uninspired, upset	Bad
Questioned my general ability		Full of doubt	Good
Questioned my commitment		Anger & resentment	Bad
Criticised me to a colleague of my level		Humiliation	Bad

It's Honesty Time:

So, on your list, you will have noted the recent situations and examples of when your DB has commented and the resulting feelings their comments evoked. You will also have noted down if you think their communication with you was ok and fair – or harsh and hurtful. At this point, I'm going to ask you to be very honest with yourself.

Have a look at the six examples of when your DB caused you annoyance, discomfort or pain. Think about each situation carefully and evaluate all of the circumstances attached to it. Try and put yourself in your boss's shoes and then, with your neutral and 'totally honest' hat on, ask yourself these two questions about each situation:

ONE: DB ACTION

'Was my boss justified in being unhappy with what I did or didn't do and were they justified in bringing this to my attention? In brief were they right... did they have a point?'

TWO: THEIR COMMUNICATION

Irrespective of if I was in the right or in the wrong, was the way my boss communicated their displeasure measured, professional and acceptable – or was it unprofessional, harsh, sarcastic, hurtful etc?

The Two Ways Bosses Cause Pain:

As you may already have worked out, fundamentally there are two ways in which your boss can get things wrong and so cause you discomfort and pain. These are as follows:

ONE:

They can assess a situation incorrectly and conclude that you have made an error and you are at fault when in fact you are not. They have got it wrong and are placing blame at your door when it is undeserved; a good example of this being if you get criticised for delivering work late when, in reality, a deadline was never established with you.

TWO:

Irrespective of whether you have made an error or not, the manner in which your boss communicates their displeasure is unprofessional, harsh and hurtful.

Now these two ways can interplay in a few different ways. Here's an example...

You have unjustly had blame put at your door for delivering work late. However, though wrong in their assessment of this, your boss did actually handle the conversation (Their Communication with you) very well. They were not aggressive and their general tone was professional and measured.

Alternatively, perhaps you did miss the deadline and your boss had a justifiable point and was right to talk to you about it, but on this occasion, they handle the conversation, the 'Communication' very badly. They were perhaps verbally aggressive, harsh and sarcastic. The let their anger show and they were far from professional and measured.

Back to the Assessment....

Please be very honest. Look at your six scenarios and be brutally truthful with yourself.

Were you late in finishing the report? Where you, in reality, rambling on like a muppet in the meeting? Are your sales figures for last month really pretty ropey? Was the idea presented in the meeting ill-conceived and badly explained? Have you lost focus and are you generally struggling with your work? Are you missing deadlines? Is your time-keeping a little sloppy? Could your attitude be better?

When you have come to your conclusions, mark them down as 'Just' or 'Unjust' in the appropriate column.

The Six Scenario Assessment is now done, but what do we think? What has this process of honest assessment confirmed?

What you are likely to find is that your assessment and answers lead you to fall into one of the following three employee groups.

The 3 Types of Employee (The 3 Groups)
GROUP A:

Having had a think about the six scenarios and having been totally honest your conclusion can perhaps be summarised as follows:

> *'You know what, on reflection perhaps I do need to pay attention to my performance and my standards at work and it's possible my boss does have a point. Also, the way the boss speaks to me is really not as harsh as I first thought. While I'm almost loath to admit it, the boss is perhaps not the ogre I thought they were.*

By definition, this will tend to be a very small group, and though you might not be in it, I hope you can appreciate that there are people out there who, having read this book thus far, will be. These Group A people have stepped back and had a really honest think about the situation and have concluded that, in reality, their boss does have a justifiable reason to occasionally complain – and you know what, their style of communication is really not too bad.

So, what is the way forward if you conclude you are a Group A person? Well, first of all, it may be good to ponder and even take comfort from the fact that your boss is not too challenging after all, but more importantly, you could perhaps help the relationship by making some small improvements to your overall performance. (At the end of this book there is a bonus chapter containing general tips on how to improve the relationship with your boss.)

Now, as for the rest of us? ...the remaining 95%...let's have a look at Groups B and C.

GROUP B:

To be a Group B person, the results of your six-question scenario will lead you to have the following general thought...

> 'Yes, I make occasional errors and my performance could be better, but there are also times when I *am* criticised unfairly. On top of this, the way my boss talks to me about my failings, be they justified or not, is at times sarcastic, cutting, demeaning and occasionally even aggressive. There is just no need to talk to me like that'.

The above type of conclusion means that there are times when your boss has justifiable reason to comment and even criticise, but these occasions are **not** too frequent at all. However, you are also very clear that there are times when the criticism you receive is simply not justified.

In addition to this, you have concluded that the way your boss talks to you is not good. Instead of bringing about an inner feeling of 'Yes, I understand and acknowledge and I want to improve' their approach and style of communication is one that evokes the negative and destructive feelings you listed in your assessment.

Now, feelings and emotions are, of course, very personal things and are different from person to person. However, communication from your DB should **not** be any of the following

So, if for whatever reason your boss makes you experience any of the above emotions then they are not communicating with you in the correct or right way. It's as simple as that!

GROUP C:

To be a Group C person, the results of your six-scenario assessment will tend to leave you thinking the following:

> *'I genuinely do a great job...So why is nothing ever good enough? Why am I criticised unfairly and why do they talk to me like that?'*

After careful and honest analysis, you feel that by and large, you do a great job, but your boss is firstly unjust in their analysis of your performance (you do a great job but they just don't see it) but, at times, they are almost downright cruel in how they communicate their unjustified criticism.

Like with Group B people, you are <u>definitely</u> justified i·
this situation and bringing some respect, some ca
fairness to the relationship.

So, to summarise, in general terms, people tend to fall into three
categories at work, defined as follows…

GROUP A PEOPLE:

Do make mistakes and perhaps too many and don't always
have the greatest of attitudes. The boss IS justified in
bringing things to their attention and perhaps on reflection
is not too unpleasant in how they do this.

GROUP B PEOPLE:

By and large, display a good attitude in the work place.
Do make <u>occasional</u> mistakes and errors but are also often
unjustly criticised. In addition, the communication is often
unprofessional/harsh etc and so evokes various negative
feelings. They would not mind being picked up on things
by their boss – but please make it civil!

GROUP C PEOPLE:

Generally do a good or even great job and display a
positive attitude to work. However, despite all of the
positives, their boss does not acknowledge them. And,
on the contrary, is overtly picky and critical. In addition
to this, the style of communication is unpleasant and so
evokes negative feelings.

Assessment over…which category did you identify with? Which
category do you fall into?

Of course, Category A requires no conversation with your DB and
indeed your DB is not too difficult at all. As we identified, a small

improvement in the quality of work will almost certainly move the relationship forward.

However, if you are in Category B or C, then the analysis has identified that you are being treated unfairly, either in your boss's assessment of you, how they talk to you – or both!

So, confident in the knowledge that we indeed have a case, let's start to think about addressing the situation and bringing about the change we SO want and so deserve!

KEY MESSAGES:

- Not everyone who thinks they have a difficult boss does.

- Before we start on the process of improving the relationship, we need to be certain we are keeping our side of the bargain and we are not creating justifiable reasons for our boss to criticise us.

- Via the Six Scenario Assessment we know for certain which group we fall into.

- If we are in Group B or Group C, we definitely have a Difficult Boss!

5
It's Time for a Change – It's Time for Action!

As well as running training courses all over the UK, I also coach people on a one-to-one basis and quite often the challenge that we discuss is exactly the one you face, namely *'My boss is unreasonable...My boss is a nightmare'*.

Normally, I get a very detailed, prolonged and graphic account of just how terrible the DB is and just how dreadful the impact is on them. They then, not unreasonably, go into detail about how they can't sleep at night, how they hate him or her, how they are constantly humiliated, how they always have their authority undermined and how they always have their ideas ignored – or worse still stolen.

However, having listened carefully and attentively, I then normally ask what I call my million-dollar question, which is...

'So, what do you plan to do about it then?'

At this point, I quite often receive a look similar to that of a person asked to jump off the Eiffel Tower with a bed sheet as a parachute, in as much as they have no belief at all that they could actually say something or do anything to bring about a positive change. I normally get a reply along the lines of:

'Well, I can't actually say anything can I?
I mean you don't know what they are like –
it's just not possible.'

Now, at this point, I do appreciate that you may have similar views and you may be pretty certain that taking action is simply not something you can contemplate. However, there are a few important things to remember.

From your own analysis, if you are in Group B or Group C, then your boss can, at times, make you feel a whole host of emotions that are unwelcome, undeserved and even unhealthy. They can have a very negative impact on you; so much so, it can occasionally impact on your health. So, with this being the case, then if you are in Group B or Group C, you simply HAVE to take action… you have to act!

With action in mind, here are two key statements that I would like you to think about and ponder…

STATEMENT ONE:

'Nothing changes unless you change it.'

STATEMENT TWO:

'Do what you have always done; get what
you've always got.'

What these two beautiful statements highlight is that unless you take action, the chances of anything ever changing are slim to say the least. Yes, a divine miracle could take place and your previously inconsiderate, rude and even verbally aggressive DB might one day wake up and decide to be the personification of Mahatma Ghandi and Mother Theresa all rolled into one – but we both know that won't happen!

Alternatively, we can sit around with our fingers crossed hoping for a change that will also never happen. Or worse still, we wait vainly hoping that that our DB will leave the company and our lives will return to normality.

Lastly, we can consider leaving the organisation ourselves so that we free ourselves of the pain and discomfort that we have to endure. But let me ask you this…is it really an option to be, in effect, driven out of our job without really trying to resolve the problem?

The answer is, of course, no and it is just and right that we step up and take action, for unless we facilitate action nothing will change at all. The misery, unhappiness, frustration and discontent that you have felt to date because of your DB will almost certainly carry on into the future, into next week, next month and next year. Nothing will change! You are unhappy and hurt now and you will be unhappy and hurt tomorrow.

So, the ball is in your court…action MUST be taken. You have a right to speak up and for your own well-being, sanity and health it is what you should do and what you need to do. However…

With taking action in mind, the real tragedy is that so many people feel that they **can't** take action. They either are not sure how to do it or they daren't do it, or both. However, via the strategies in this book both of these challenges can be overcome, and overcome more easily than you ever imagined possible.

So, the message is this…

Via your own analysis, you now have a clear answer to the question *'Am I really the victim of a DB?'* If you are in Group B or Group C, you most definitely are and you have a justifiable reason to bring about a change in your DB.

You know they are unfair, unreasonable and downright unjust. However, and more importantly, you also know that they are not likely to wake up one morning and have changed into the boss of your dreams. They will continue to act just as they always have, so you HAVE to take action and bring about a change in them.

The real joy of this?...It is not difficult at all!

So, please start to open the door of possibility and get happy with the idea that you CAN and WILL sit down and have 'that conversation' with your boss, no matter how impossible it may have felt in the past, because, via the strategies and techniques in this book you will understand that it really is VERY easy...if you know how...and soon you will!

KEY MESSAGES:

- Unless you take action, nothing will change. Your boss will continue to treat you as they treat you now. The frustration, discomfort and pain will continue.

- You have a justifiable cause and reason to talk to them about things.

- You CAN do this.

- Doing so WILL bring about the changes you desire.

6
Understanding Your Boss:

'Try & Understand My Boss?...
You Have To Be Kidding'

In the next chapter, Chapter 7, we will look in detail at <u>exactly</u> how we Manage Up, and so bring about the changes that you seek.

We will look at the special approaches we will use when we do finally address the issues with our DB and we will discover that by understanding and applying just one simple technique, they will listen and take on board what we say. However, before we do this it might benefit us if we take a few moments to try and understand our boss.

Now at this point you are probably thinking *'Mmmm...how do you understand someone like them'* but understanding the person in the other corner is always a good thing and it always enhances communication, for remember, Managing Up is <u>all</u> about communication.

The first thing to acknowledge is that while they might indeed be challenging, rude, arrogant, bad-mannered, abrasive and downright difficult, they <u>are</u> the boss, and with this comes responsibility and almost certainly a good degree of pressure.

Of course, in the perfect world, this is not your problem and it's true they are paid to take the pressure that goes with the job. However, understanding that your DB has challenges of their own might just help us understand them and so communicate with them better.

So yes, they may strut about like Attila the Hun with a migraine but who is to say that they are not feeling a whole lot of the emotions that we ourselves feel at times? Yes, they might look supremely confidant and never ask or take advice from you but could it not be possible that deep inside they have their own insecurities, doubts, fears and demons?

So, when they are being difficult, a good strategy is to try and step back and ask yourself the following question:

> *'Why are they like this…*
> *what is driving their behaviour?'*

You see, trying to get an understanding of what they are going through and how they themselves are feeling is not a bad thing. Also, don't forget, they may have a very difficult and challenging boss too!

This particular phenomenon is more common than you may think and often their poor style of leadership and communication is all they know, as they have no role model other than their own bad boss!

Another big factor in how they behave is the possibility that they have found themselves in a job that they have not had training for.

A study by CareerBuilder.com identified that a huge 58% of managers said they had received no management training at all. In addition, many managers did not even set out to be a manager, but instead found it almost thrust upon them in their quest to do well and be a success in their career.

They perhaps trained as an accountant, an IT engineer or they worked in sales and were good at what they did, so much so they got promoted and became a 'Manager'. So, in a lot of cases, bosses have been promoted to the job because they were good at what they <u>used</u> to do, and not because they are good at managing people and helping people who work for them be more effective.

This one statistic could make us all run for the hills as the reality is that there are a huge number of managers who simply have not been trained in how to manage. They are what are often called 'Accidental Managers' – and I speak from personal experience when I say it's a scary experience to discover that your manager doesn't actually know how to be one!

So, for a moment, try and step into the shoes of the boss. They may indeed be all of the things that make your life so stressful – but they are human.

Now, again, I can almost hear some of you talking back to me and saying *'No...No...No...they are definitely not human'* – but despite whatever you think of them, they are not too different from me and you; it's just that perhaps they don't choose to show it.

So, with this 'Are they human?' dilemma in mind, here's an experience that happened to me a few years ago that had a major impact on how I viewed all unreasonable and aggressive people.

Enter Mr Unpleasant!

About 20 years ago, I was having a meeting with a Managing Director of a company that I was trying to sell to. While he was not my boss, he had all of the characteristics of a DB. He was arrogant, overbearing, didn't listen, mildly offensive and very dismissive of me. In brief, he was a pretty unpleasant man who seemed to be on a crusade to make me feel humiliated, weak and worthless.

I had been warned that Mr Unpleasant was difficult and he certainly was – but he was a potential customer and a big one at that, so I was hanging on in there and trying not to let his sarcastic and critical comments hurt too much.

The first part of the meeting was exactly as I had been warned and I witnessed a man full of his own importance and a bully to boot. However, before my very eyes this changed.

In mid-rant, his secretary rang through to say that his daughter was here to see him with some form of package. For the first time ever, he showed me some civility and asked if we could put the meeting on hold for a couple of minutes while his daughter popped in to quickly hand something over. I, of course, agreed.

What he didn't know was that his daughter was accompanied by her daughter: Mr Unpleasant's granddaughter – who, I later discovered, was aged five. On being shown into his huge office his daughter, seeing her father had a guest, immediately apologised for interrupting. However, five-year-olds are not too keen to display such correctness and on seeing her grandfather, she ran across the floor in a fit of excitement shouting *'Hello Granddad...I have been shopping with Mummy'* and threw herself into his arms.

At this point, I half expected Mr Unpleasant to callously step aside and allow the child to crash to the floor, but before my eyes he changed beyond recognition and became the gentlest, most loving, caring and compassionate granddad you could imagine.

He scooped the obviously much adored five-year-old into his arms and within seconds, she was sat on his knee looking across the desk at me.

Observing an admittedly adorable five-year-old rearrange Mr Unpleasant's desk, as she commanded *'Come on, Granddad – let's play offices'* – was something of a joy and it was as if a miracle had taken place. She created new piles of papers, re-organised his tub of pens and generally took over – before announcing with a giggle, *'I'm going to mess up your hair, Grandad'* – which she duly did!

Within three minutes she was gone, but not before she had planted one very sloppy kiss all over his cheek and again scuffed up his hair for good measure.

When she had departed, he, of course, apologised for the mini tornado that had been his granddaughter but, having witnessed the other side of Mr Unpleasant and having seen how much he enjoyed the interaction with his granddaughter, I honestly thought the barriers would remain down and the truly lovely granddad I had witnessed would prevail. How wrong I was, for within thirty seconds he had composed himself and pretty quickly returned to his previous obnoxious self.

But you know what, from that day on Mr Unpleasant was never quite the scary and foreboding character that I had first found him to be and from then on, whenever I met him, I always saw him differently!

I did go on to do a considerable amount of business with Mr Unpleasant and he pretty much remained just that, unpleasant – but somehow the intervention of his five-year-old granddaughter and the transformation she brought about in him helped me to see a very different side of his personality.

So, what's the message here?

Well, whatever your DB is like, chances are they have their 'granddaughter moments', moments when they display a side of their personality that IS human, that IS compassionate, that IS caring and that IS thoughtful. In brief, away from the pressure cooker of work, chances are they are a pretty decent person; yes, perhaps not all of the time but certainly some of the time and if we can keep this image in the back of our minds, it will help us to understand them.

Of course, chances are they don't have a five-year-old granddaughter to bring out their better side but perhaps there's a much loved and respected partner, a parent, a son, a daughter, a grandparent or a dog, or a cat.

Whoever and whatever it is, there is a good chance that, at times, your DB is actually a pretty reasonable if not downright nice person and if we can TRY and understand and acknowledge this, and indeed even imagine it happening, then this will help in our relationship with our DB. (As a side thought, whenever I used to be on the receiving end of Mr Unpleasant's aggression, I always used to imagine him crawling around his lounge floor with his granddaughter on his back shouting *'Gee Up, Granddad'* – This thought always helped!)

So, the moral is....

Yes, they may be bad but they are not bad all the time. They love their wife, children, grandparents, mum and dad, dog, cat or pet hamster – and seeing Mr Unpleasant playing offices with his five-year-old granddaughter made me realise this.

So, try and understand your DB. Understand that they have pressure, disappointment, frustration, anger, upset and even perhaps heartache. Of course, it is not right or justified that they take these emotions out on you – but simply understanding that they have challenges just like us, and by trying to understand 'where they are coming from' will help the relationship with them.

Last but not least, remember that they are human. Yes, I know at the office or your place of work there is little evidence of this but in their private moments, they are! Try and understand this and truly acknowledge it and it will help.

KEY MESSAGES:

- Trying to understand your boss is a good thing and will help the process.

- While, in many ways, they may indeed be unreasonable… they are human.

- They themselves will undoubtedly have challenges, pressures and stress.

- Yes, at times they may be an unpleasant human being – but this is not the real them! Away from work, they are a nice person.

7
'Let's Talk'… Having 'That' Conversation with Your Boss

So, this is where we are:

- We have identified that if you are on the receiving end of DB behaviour. If they are high on the scale, then your life can be made a total misery, and if not a misery certainly unpleasant or at least frustrating.

- We have also stepped back and had a close examination of the working relationship with our boss, the objective being to calmly and analytically assess if we are justified in feeling we are badly treated by them. If we have got this far, the conclusion is yes, we are. Therefore, we either fall into Group B or Group C. In either case, we have a justifiable right and a need to try and change and improve things.

- In addition, we have also understood that unless we take action, little if anything will change and our Difficult Boss will continue to be just that…DIFFICULT. The pain, humiliation, anger, upset and distress that you feel will continue – unless, of course, we do something about it!

- Finally, we have had a look at trying to understand our boss, for no matter how onerous, de-motivating, cold, unappreciative and hurtful they may be, there is almost certainly another side to them and unless we appreciate this, we will struggle to even think we can change them. They are human!

So, against this background, we now arrive at the main part of this book, the main part of the journey that will explain how you can bring some calm, respect and understanding to the relationship with your DB, the part that explains to you just how to have that 'perfect' conversation that goes just how you want it to, and so brings about the positive change in your boss's behaviour that you seek.

For ease of reading, this all-important section of the book is split into five very important sections or Building Bricks. For the purpose of reading, these Building Bricks should be seen as mini chapters. Of the five building bricks, brick number two is both the most lengthy and detailed – so take your time with this and work through it page by page. The five building bricks are:

1. Confidentiality

2. Preparation & Content

3. Delivery

4. Choosing the Moment

5. Your Attitude & Frame of Mind

Now, before we look at Brick Number One, let's understand one thing that is absolutely fundamental to the entire process contained in this book.

The whole basis of changing your DB into a GB (Good Boss) is centred on one thing, and that is that you take action and have an actual conversation with them where you explain and discuss the situation and the changes you would like to see.

Now, again at this point, I can almost hear the screams of *'No I can't do that'* or *'No way...I have tried that and it didn't work at all'* – but please believe me, you can.

The reason why? ...because this time the conversation will be structured differently to any other that you have had and it will contain one key ingredient that was probably missing from all previous conversations.

So, please stick with me and have faith that by the time you get to the end of this book, you will clearly understand and know the following:

> **WHY** your conversation will work.

> **WHY** you will feel confident in having the conversation.

> **WHEN** the right time to have it is.

> **WHAT** to say.

> **HOW** you will say it.

And most important of all...

> ***WHY*** your DB will agree with you and so make a positive change in their behaviour.

Sound a tall order? Well, it's not. Let's look at the first of the required building bricks.

Building Brick One: Confidentiality

Many years ago, I worked in retailing and was an Area Manager controlling 15 fashion stores. One of the stores was managed by a lady who I will call Val. Now I thought Val and I got on just fine. We had a good, honest and open working relationship and I felt happy that, all in all, she was happy with my style of management and that she was more than ok with me being her boss. In brief, I thought I was a GB and that if Val had any complaints or gripes, she would address them with me.

On this particular day, I had visited the store in the morning and left at lunchtime to go to another store 20 miles away. Val thanked me for the visit and bid me a cheery goodbye and I left the store comfortable that all was well in our relationship.

No more than a minute out of the door, I realised I had left my car keys in Val's office and so returned. I walked back through the shop, but just as I was about to open the door, I heard Val on the phone to the manager at my next store of destination giving her a tip off that I was on my way, but more alarmingly for me, also sharing her views and opinions about me. On hearing this conversation, I rightly or wrongly hesitated at the door and listened.

I have to be honest and say that what she was saying was nothing too scathing or bad and it was a mixture of comments about the 'personal me' and my performance as her boss. However, hearing that, in her opinion, I had no idea how to colour coordinate merchandise, that I could not choose a shirt and tie that matched to save my life, that I made lots of promises that I simply forgot about and that I needed a good haircut did little for either my professional or personal confidence, let alone my self-esteem.

Of course, the conversation was a personal one and wrongly I had eavesdropped so, of course, I made the decision not to mention anything about my discovery.

However, although I tried to put the comments to the back of my mind and continue in my quest to be a GB, my pride, my vanity, but also my feelings had been hurt. The weakness here was, of course, all mine, but nevertheless as a result of Val's conversation I always struggled to see our relationship in its previous good light.

The reason for this story?

No one likes to be talked about behind their back and your boss is no different. While you might feel they deserve it (and they might), it is unprofessional and disrespectful, but more importantly it can get you into trouble and can seriously hinder your objective, which is to have a private one-to-one confidential conversation with them that goes well.

Idle chat around the office and workplace about how *'Jenny is going to talk to him you know'* or how *'Steve is going to sort it out'* is not a good thing in any eventuality and if your boss gets to hear about your pending approach, it could be disastrous.

While, of course, you might choose to confide in a partner or loved one at home, or even a close friend, I would advise you never to discuss your strategy and forthcoming approach to your boss with your colleagues in general. Yes, in extreme circumstances perhaps confide in one close friend at work but if you do, you need to make sure you have 100% belief in their confidentiality. If your boss hears on the grapevine about your unhappiness with them and that you plan to 'have it out with them', it will do little to foster a fair hearing.

Of course, this is a very simple piece of advice but having been a boss you would be amazed just how much stuff we do hear.

The bottom line is you are going to have a very serious and important conversation with your DB, a conversation that can greatly improve your working relationship and so your life.

Therefore, DON'T jeopardise it by idle and unprofessional gossip around the workplace. It's unprofessional and it's just not worth it!

KEY MESSAGES:

- Keep your plans and intentions to talk to your boss to yourself.

- Never make the pending conversation with your boss common gossip around the workplace.

- If you have to confide in someone, try and make it with a loved one or close friend who is away from your place of work.

- If you do share your intentions with a colleague, make sure their confidentiality is guaranteed.

Building Brick Two: Preparation & Content (the BIG Brick!)

When most people finally pluck up enough courage to talk to their DB about the situation, it normally fails for one or more of several reasons, all of which are linked to failing to acknowledge the importance of the five building bricks.

Key reasons for the conversation going badly are:

- They have been indiscreet and their DB has rumbled their intentions. As a result, their DB is almost on the defensive before the conversation has even taken place.

- They have failed to prepare properly, and the so content of the conversation is very poor.

- They are in the wrong frame of mind – the two most common incorrect mind-sets being extreme anger, normally after being on the receiving end of a particularly bad experience with a boss, or extreme anxiety, when they have become so nervous about the conversation they cannot function properly and so can't deliver their conversation as they wanted.

- Alternatively, they chose the wrong moment to have the conversation and have either responded with a knee jerk reaction to the aforementioned DB outburst of hostility (this normally leads to an argument and even more DB aggression) – or they have chosen a moment when their DB is simply not for listening. Needless to say, both of these are not good.

As you can see, getting the building bricks of success in place is essential and all are vital, but the importance of Preparation & Content cannot be underestimated and it is in this section that the magic ingredient of success – the thing that will make the conversation work – is created and put in place.

To start to explain just what the magic ingredient is, it is worth taking a moment to examine what a badly prepared conversation might look like. Now, of course, there are many different ways to get it wrong and indeed you may have unwittingly already tried one or more of these, but let's just use a very simple example that hopefully contains the essence of how not to do it.

Shamela has worked for Mr Jones for six months. He is at the extreme end of the Difficult Scale and, understandably, she hates his aggressive, ungrateful and mildly bullying approach. Shamela can take it no longer and decides to talk to him. The conversation goes a little like this:

> *'Mr Jones – I do need to have a talk to you. Have you got a moment? I have worked with you for six months now and during that time I have always tried my best, but despite this, quite often you have been very unappreciative and at times very de-motivational. Yes, I know that you are busy and under pressure but sometimes the way you talk to me is very upsetting and really not fair.*
>
> *I do want to keep working for you and I love the company, but I do feel that it would be better and fair if you could acknowledge my work a little more, not swear at me and generally be a little more civil'.*

The above is a very simplistic way of putting things and, as stated, there are many ways of wording this type of conversation, but whatever way Shamela says it, she is correct. Mr Jones <u>is</u>

unappreciative, de-motivational and aggressive and in a nutshell, he is a difficult and unreasonable man.

So, the big question is: Will Shamela's approach work? Will her conversation with Mr Jones bring about the change in his behaviour she seeks?

Well, the answer to that is that if Mr Jones was a reasonable and decent man it may well do and if your boss has these qualities then just plucking up the courage to let them know your true feelings could well be all that is needed (this specific type of conversation, with the boss who is actually not too bad at all, is covered in Bonus Chapter 2). However, from what Shamela has said, Mr Jones does not appear to be this type of character and her conversation with him highlighted that he is more than challenging on several fronts.

So, the answer to the question 'Will her chat work?' is almost certainly a no!

The reason...

It is because she has based all of her request for better behaviour from Mr Jones on one thing – namely an appeal to his better nature. But of course, being the archetypal DB who is at the high end of the scale his better nature is somewhat well hidden.

The conclusion is that using any approach similar to the above has a high chance of failure. So, have a look again at the structure and content of Shamela's conversation and then ask yourself this all-important question...

WHAT'S IN IT FOR MR JONES?

Yes, all of Shamela's comments are absolutely true and 100% correct and so her requests are justified and reasonable. However, we have to understand and acknowledge that while she may be right and Mr Jones is wrong, he is the boss and, as such, has the upper hand.

So this one simple acknowledgement and understanding really underlines the key point of the conversation with your DB.

Yes, it would be wonderful if just because we asked them to change, they did so and so became the fair, inspirational and considerate boss we all desire. However, the reality is that if by nature they are unreasonable, selfish and self-absorbed then in their eyes they probably have no need, inclination or reason to change...**UNLESS, OF COURSE, WE GIVE THEM A REASON!**

A Little Bit More about Bosses in General:

Now, at any given time in the world, there will be hundreds of thousands – if not millions of bosses – so generalisation is, of course, dangerous – but let's go down that road and generalise a little anyway.

It is probably fair to say that of all the bosses out there, some will be great and a real pleasure to work for and some will be good, in as much as they create little if any pain and discomfort amongst the people who work for them. However, in my experience, most bosses do carry a degree of selfishness and a certain self-centred streak, although often they justify this with such statements as *'I need to be tough to get the job done'* or *'I haven't got time to be nice'*.

To some small degree this approach and these characteristics and traits can be useful for a boss and we should always remember that in most instances, bosses <u>do</u> indeed have to get the job done and they <u>do</u> have to deliver the goods. However, too much of a self-centred approach is not beneficial to great leadership.

So, what are the characteristics of the person we refer to as the boss? Well as already mentioned, there are a lot of them out there and every one of them is different, but quite often a boss is a pretty driven and ambitious person. They display a strong desire to get things done, they want solutions and not problems, they hate things going wrong, they do not like being criticised, they are very ambitious, they seek efficiency and generally want to be seen as successful and a star!

Of course, it is equally possible that your DB falls into the totally opposite camp, in as much as they are fundamentally lazy and want to do as little as possible but still claim the glory. While this type of DB is not too common, they are out there and their unreasonable and unfair behaviour is often dispensed as part of their defence and camouflage strategy. In brief, they do not want to be found out and so fire off all manner of bluster and unreasonable requests in an attempt to retain their cover.

However, both display the same characteristics as mentioned but for different reasons – and while these characteristics can be common to most people, it is normally the case that any person who levitates to the position of boss has some, if not all of them, and often at a potency that can be verging on the unhealthy!

Therefore the general conclusion is that, at times, the archetypal DB is a selfish 'so and so' who sees things predominantly from their perspective.

So what we discovered with Shamela's example is that when dealing with this type of person we need to give them a reason or a 'benefit' to change. By definition, taking an approach that hopefully appeals to their better nature and their wish for fair play will simply not work, as they are short in both of these qualities.

In brief, the conversation we have with our boss needs to be constructed in a way that acknowledges their personality and their approach to their work. It needs to immediately contain 'something for them' – it needs to have a magic ingredient of success!

Enter the Magic Ingredient ...
Enter 'The Benefit Statement'

As we have identified, if your boss is a reasonable human being then just letting them know your true feelings will probably be enough to bring about a positive change, and I would absolutely urge you to have this conversation (Again, please see Bonus Chapter 2 for specific guidance on this type of boss). However, if your DB is just that – difficult – then the conversation that you have with them MUST contain a benefit or a reward for them changing, otherwise it's unlikely they will!

Of course, in the perfect world, it would be nice if we didn't have to apply such tactics to bring about the change in behaviour that we seek – but when the person we are dealing with is fundamentally unreasonable, then we do have to apply a little persuasion and guile. So, again, can I stress that this is not us being scheming or manipulative – but us simply understanding that a certain approach and style of communication is needed.

Having discovered with Shamela's conversation the type of approach that <u>won't</u> work, let's have a look at the sort of things we should we be saying.

This is the scenario:

Imagine you are about to commence the all- important conversation with your DB. The first thing you have to do is grab their attention and their interest as without this, the conversation will probably go nowhere.

We therefore we need to open the conversation with something that does not lead them to think *'Here we go – It's Shamela moaning again'* – but instead gets them thinking and feeling that the conversation that is about to happen may actually be of benefit to them.

So, the conversation needs to open with a Benefit for them – so that they do engage with you and they do listen. Then, with their full attention gained you have the platform to explain how they can obtain better performance from you if they just managed you a little differently. They hear this and conclude that a change in their behaviour might actually be a good thing after all as <u>they</u> will get something out of it.

Therefore the big message here is to understand that to get the positive outcome we desire we need to start the conversation by immediately tempting them with an opening BENEFIT STATEMENT.

Why Benefit Statements Work:

As you start to think about how to construct your Benefit Statement, it is interesting and indeed pleasantly ironic to note that its success and effectiveness is likely to be helped considerably by the very characteristics that you perhaps dislike about your DB.

We know already that as an example, the typical DB seeks efficiency, wants to be seen to be successful and doesn't want things going wrong and it is this desire for success and acknowledgement that will make your benefit statement sound oh so appealing to them!

A Benefit Statement is, in effect, a fairly simple statement that does not have to be overly wordy or complex and it does not have to be overly generous in terms of what it offers. It does not need to be offering the world via extra hours or excessive pandering, but it does have to offer a tangible benefit to the boss.

In brief, the Benefit Statement is about creating a deal or an agreement with your DB. They treat you in a fairer, more agreeable, more humane and acceptable manner and they stop the excessive nit picking. They ease off on the micro-managing, they cease the sarcastic comments and they start to actually listen to you etc.

In general, they stop doing the things that cause you frustration, distress and even pain and, in return, they get improved performance from you.

But where does this improved performance come from?

Well this question, but more importantly its answer (and the process of you buying into the answer) is vitally important to the success of the conversation you will have with your DB. So let's take a few moments to appreciate and understand a few key fundamentals based around how as humans we operate and function, and what is called the science of improved performance.

Let's start by asking the question again …

Where does the improved performance come from?

Well the answer actually lies in another question, namely…

Does the way your boss currently manages you bring out your best performance?

It's in answering this question that the improved performance lies.

The Science of Improved Performance:

Here is a scenario to consider:

Imagine that a magic wand has been waved and, starting tomorrow, you have a new boss, a boss who is considerate, understanding, helpful, supportive, motivating, trusting, fun, empowering and inspiring – a boss who is there for you, who values you, who treats you well. This is a boss who gets rid of the pressure cooker atmosphere that makes you feel you are always walking on eggshells and replaces it with an environment that has fairness and calm at its heart. In brief you really like your new boss and it's a pleasure and a joy to work for them.

If this was the case then ask yourself this important question. Would you naturally, and almost without having to try become one or more of the following…

More Productive	More Efficient
More Creative	More Willing
More Hardworking	More Dedicated
More Enthusiastic	More Keen
More Conscientious	More Effective
More Empowered	More Motivated

When I am doing one-to-one work with people about their difficult boss and I ask this question, the response is nearly always a resounding 'Yes' to most, if not all of the options. But why?

Well at the heart of the answer is that mysterious and sometimes elusive thing called **motivation**.

It is generally accepted that when we have to deal with the aforementioned sarcastic comments, excessive nit picking, micro-managing and general harsh and unfair behaviour then our level of natural motivation diminish.   With this in mind here is another question to ask yourself:

'How Motivated Does Your DB's Behaviour Make You Feel?

The chances are the answer is 'not very much' or 'not at all'

So the answer to the question 'Where does the improved performance come from' lies in the basis of how we fundamentally operate as humans.

It is a proven and accepted fact that in the vast majority of cases people naturally perform better and at a higher standard if they are motivated – and when we are in this state of mind we generally find that we crack on and get things done – and generally to a high standard too. However, when we have low levels of motivation, or are 'de-motivated' then we find we really struggle to summon up the energy, will power and enthusiasm to do just about anything really well.

So what sort of things lead us to feeling de-motivated?

Well in general terms all sorts of things can trigger a sudden decline in our mood…and so our levels of motivation – but in the work place it is acknowledged that things like excessive pressure, unfair criticism, lack of praise, aggressive communication, lack of general care, lack of understanding, unclear expectations, subtle psychological stress, mild or even blatant bullying and fear of failure are all massive de-motivators. More importantly though it is also acknowledged that when these destructive and negative influences are taken away then all of the things on the list on the previous page naturally kick in and performance soars.

So motivation, or in this instance de-motivation, is a major influencer of how we perform at work – but for anyone who doubts this concept then we only have to look at the world of sport.

Yes, it is acknowledged that some of the world's top sports coaches and managers can drive great performances from their players via the issuing of demanding challenges, tough and often critical comments – and more than the odd rant! However, if they take things too far then instead of motivating their players the very opposite happens.

As an example a top soccer player, cyclist, swimmer or athlete etc can become totally paralysed by the effects of fear, humiliation and excessive criticism from their coach or manager. On the same theme, a truly great footballer can almost shrink in size, loose all confidence and almost hide away on the pitch if the crowd start to get on their back.

However, change the coach or manager from someone who is fundamentally unfair, overtly critical, harsh, uncaring and generally demotivating, to a new coach who is inspiring, interested, under-standing and fair – and improvement follows naturally WITHOUT the sports person having to train harder or even try harder. In brief, it just happens naturally, as a result of a more harmonious stress-free working relationship that has motivation and NOT de-motivation at its core.

So, imagine if you had your new amazing boss. Would you walk into your place of work with a cheery attitude? Would you feel like you could operate without feeling you are walking on the proverbial eggshells all the time? Would you be more motivated? Would you generally feel like cracking on with your job, safe in the knowledge that that you are not going to be unfairly criticised at any given moment? Would you get more done? Would you be more productive? Would you be just generally better?

Now if your thinking resembles anything near a 'Yes' to these questions then you now understand just how the deal with your DB will work. In brief, it can be summarised as follows.

ONE:

You know your boss would welcome and like more creativity, general efficiency, fewer mistakes, more initiative from you (i.e. whatever it is you think **your** particular boss would think 'Oh Yes Please' to).

TWO:

You know in your heart that if your DB was less sarcastic, hurtful, rude and demotivating and critical and were more acknowledging and supportive then, by definition, you would naturally feel more comfortable at work. Your levels of motivation would increase and so your performance would flourish accordingly and you would naturally deliver the things they want.

Consequently this explains the 'deal' and why it will work. You start a conversation with a Benefit Statement. Your DB realises there is something in it for them and so engages and listens, and tempted by the offer of naturally improved performance, they see there is real benefit for them to change.

This entire strategy is based on the understanding that while they are currently going about it in all the wrong way, your boss does actually want the very best performance from you.

Now, at times, it might appear that they are simply going out of their way to bully and hurt and yes it might seem as if it's all just sport to them. However, ultimately, they do want the best performance from you as a great performance from you of course looks good for them and helps them succeed. So, what the process just described does is to get them to see that the way they are going about it at the moment is totally wrong and it's actually having the exact opposite effect!

Your side of the bargain, namely your increased and improved performance is NOT achieved by you having to put in an abundance of increased hours, harder work and more effort – but more by your levels of motivation naturally increasing- and taking your general performance along with it, and all of this occurring as a result of the removal of the negative and performance inhibiting attitude of your DB.

In brief, they cut out some specific poor behaviour that is causing you pain, and in return, you naturally feel more relaxed at work. The oppression is removed; you flourish and so deliver better performance.

Understanding the concept of the science of improved performance is really important and it is one that is borne out by both extensive research, as well as my own personal experience of helping people deal with a very difficult boss. However, while we understand that our improved performance tends to happen quite naturally (when our DB starts to treat us better) that is not to say that delivering some very real 'boss benefits' is not a bad thing either, and certainly in the immediate days and weeks after the conversation.

With this idea in mind, and to help the new relationship along post conversation, are there perhaps one or two tangible things that you could now deliver, things that you previously could and would have done IF your boss had not made you feel so de-motivated, uninspired and fed up? If there are, then cracking on and delivering them post conversation with your boss may well be a very smart move.

Again though I must stress, these are not things that require you to work late or work at the weekend. However, delivering a few small 'boss benefits' …things that will make them think 'Wow thank you' will help demonstrate to your DB that the bargain is not only working for you – but for them too!

Constructing Your Benefit Statement:

Now, of course, the Benefit Statement that you use will need to be devised by you and by definition it will be unique to you. The situation that you find yourself in needs a specific approach that matches both individual circumstances and, of course, the characteristics and personality of your boss.

Devising your benefit statement will take time and care and should not be rushed. Get it right and you will immediately engage your boss and get them listening to you, as opposed to them wanting to get you out of their offices ASAP! Get it right and you are in with a great chance of success.

How long should this preparation take? Well of course I cannot say, but as a guide, if it took thirty to ninety minutes of quiet contemplation then so be it. It's the key to the conversation and it's the key to success, so take your time and get it spot on.

The next question is, what does a Benefit Statement look like?

As we have just said they are all individual to the specific situation concerned but, to help you along the way, here are a few generic examples.

> 'Helen, thanks for seeing me. I have been having a think about things and about how I could be more productive around here. If there was a way, a method, where my general efficiency improved and I even made fewer of those errors that I'm sometimes prone to – well I wonder if that would be of interest?'

> 'Mrs Anderson, if we could get to a situation where we generally communicated a whole lot better, so that I was doing more of what you really want me to do, would that generally make things better between us?'

'Helen, I have been thinking about things…if I could work in a way where I was more efficient and effective… would that help you deliver the big objective you are tasked with?'

'Mr Jones…would you like to get more out of me. More work, more projects more efficiency?'

'David, if I could highlight to you a way in which my general efficiency improved and I made fewer mistakes, well would that help you and be a positive for you?

'Mrs Udowe, if I could find a way to become a little more creative, and started to come up with my own initiatives, which I think is what you want, would that help you and the department?'

'I have been having a think about things and I'm fairly sure I could do a better job around here and be more X, Y or Z. Could I share what I'm thinking?'

As you will see, all of the above Benefit Statements will by definition gain a 'YES' answer from your boss because straight away they can see there is something in it for them. Then, with their attention gained, you can move into general conversation that is based around how you can deliver more, **IF** they managed you a little differently.

In Chapter 8, we will look in detail at how we continue the conversation via a simple 4 Stage Process once we have delivered the Benefit Statement, but whatever your Benefit Statement is, it of course needs to be delivered in the most effective way possible.

With this in mind, I accept that on the written page the Benefit Statement examples can look a little wooden, a little contrived and very scripted. So, let's move on and have a look at how we actually deliver the all-important words.

KEY MESSAGES:

- If your boss is at the high end of the Difficult Scale, their better nature is probably well hidden. Having a conversation that appeals to it probably won't work.

- Therefore, when we start the conversation with our boss, it needs to start with a Benefit Statement.

- Benefit Statements work as they immediately highlight a positive for your boss, a benefit.

- A Benefit Statement sets out the idea and the concept of a 'deal'. Your boss treats you better and in return, you deliver more/better quality work.

- The 'more/better quality work' occurs naturally as a result of the improved behaviour from your boss. This improved behaviour naturally increases your levels of motivation. It is not about you having to 'give' more.

- Take time and care to construct your Benefit Statement. Get it right and it can be life changing.

Building Brick Three: Delivery…How to Say It

Perhaps a good place to start this little mini chapter on Delivery is with the well-known saying…

> *'It's not what you say but the way that you say it.'*

These famous twelve words have never been more important than when we sit down to have the conversation with our DB, because while the content of our conversation is vital, the delivery (i.e. saying it just how we want to) is also essential. So, let's have a look at a few tips on how we can bring the scripted words to life and deliver our message with maximum impact.

The first thing to acknowledge is that the advice and guidance on delivery does, of course, have to be fairly generic. Everyone who reads this book is an individual, as is every DB. Add to this the fact that as human beings, we all have our unique and individual style of communication and you will see that what is comfortable and natural for one person feels awkward and very unnatural to another. Therefore, against this backdrop, it would be wrong for this book to suggest that there is just one way and one way only to deliver your message.

The great Oscar Wilde said 'Be yourself – everyone else is taken' and being yourself when you have the conversation with your boss is definitely the right approach. Be the real you and be the authentic you, as heartfelt sincere communication in your own particular style will be infinitely more powerful than trying to adopt the persona of someone you are not. However, that is not to say that you can't hone and sharpen your own style in a dramatic way.

So, to assist with this, here are some tips, techniques and advice to help ensure that your DB conversation is delivered with maximum effectiveness. Firstly, let's have a look at how we communicate as human beings.

Here are some interesting statistics.

How We Communicate:

When in a face-to-face, one-to-one situation we communicate in three ways. These are:

Content
(the words we say)

Tone of Voice
(how we say them)

Body Language
(our facial expressions, gestures and posture)

You might be surprised to know that when we apply some percentages of importance to each method, the research reveals the following:

Content	10%
Tone of Voice	15%
Body Language	75%

While this might initially appear a little scary, it must be said that in certain situations, these statistics can and do vary dramatically and certainly when you talk to your DB, the content percentage will be a lot higher. However, that is not to say that your body language, your 'non-verbal communication' will not be vital to the success of the conversation.

In a moment we will look at the voice, the vocal side of the conversation, but first a detailed look at the type of Body Language we need to adopt.

Body Language:

Body Language is a fairly complex topic, but you don't need to become a Professor of Body Language to make a noticeable improvement and so really up your power of communication.

In respect of Body Language, this needs to be what is called neutral, in as much as it is neither aggressive nor overly passive. Here are a few things to pay attention to.

- Sitting to have the conversation is advised as towering over your boss while declaring *'I want to have a conversation with you'* will only put your boss on the defensive.

- While it is not always an easy thing to achieve, having the conversation seated, but <u>not</u> directly facing them across their desk (or any desk) will help. Desks create barriers to communication and we want this to be a barrier-free zone. If you are fortunate enough to be able to talk at a round/circular meeting table then do so. If not, try to perch yourself at the corner of the desk so that you are not directly squaring up to each other.

- When sitting in the chair, sit back comfortably and naturally. However, excessive leaning back can send a message of either arrogance or that of being ultra 'laid back' in your approach. Both of these are undesirable. Alternatively, while it can display earnestness, leaning forward can also be perceived as overly assertive. Therefore, adopt a natural upright position and if possible, have your chair turned slightly to the side so as to avoid a front on conversation (which is, again, slightly aggressive).

- You may or may not be nervous as you start the conversation but whatever your mood, try not to fidget. Fidgeting normally sends a message of anxiousness – and we want to come across as calm, relaxed, in control and professional.

- At all times keep your arms unfolded, especially when your boss is talking. In addition (and if at all possible), try to ensure that your boss does not cross his or her arms. Research shows that agreement is rarely reached when one or both parties have folded arms.

- Last but not least, establish eye contact, but do not fix your boss with a hypnotic manic stare as this DEFINITELY will not help! However, confident eye contact sends out a message of just that… confidence!

Of course, you might be excused for thinking that all of the above is extremely fundamental stuff and, to some degree, it is. However, if we acknowledge that the majority of communication is non-verbal, you will appreciate how important it is.

In addition, remember you will be communicating with your boss via body language long before you have even opened your mouth. To support this fact, and as a point of interest when people come to sit across from my desk to talk to me, I normally have a pretty good idea of the type of conversation I am in for well before they open their mouths. That's the power of Body Language!

Tone of Voice:

Having ensured we have got our body language right when we actually start to speak, we need to be ourselves and pretty much talk as we normally talk. Adopting some alien style of verbal communication in an effort to be more assertive and dominant will do nothing for rapport building.

Unlike with body language, there is less scope for radical improvement with our voice but there are still some important things to consider. Here are a few tips.

- Preparation is all important and this cannot be overemphasised. So, when you have worked out your opening Benefit Statement and the subsequent key parts of the conversation, as set out in the following chapter, then run through them and PRACTICE! This practice can, of course, be on your own or even with a loved one but, as we discovered in the section on Confidentiality, be very careful about using a colleague to practice in front of – and, of course, <u>never</u> practice at work.

  Yes, I agree that practicing a few sentences out loud might, at first, appear and feel unnatural and mildly embarrassing but is it not true that the conversation you are going to have with your boss could well be the most important of the year! With this in mind, is it not worth committing quality time to practicing exactly what you want to say and how you want to say it… so that when the moment comes, it is delivered just how you want it to be. The big message here? …Practice is essential!

- Making a good start is key as this helps build confidence. In the next two building bricks we will look in detail at both choosing the right moment to have the conversation, but also how to adopt the right mind set, this so that we are at our most confident and best. However, the best way to build confidence is to start well. The best way to start well is to practice and prepare, and one great tip is to memorise SPECIFICALLY your opening couple of statements.

- When we are anxious or nervous, we naturally tend to talk quicker and, in most instances, this sends a negative signal that we are indeed a little tense. When practising, pay particular attention to maintaining a slightly slower than normal delivery, not so slow that it is tedious – but slow enough to send a message that you are focused and purposeful.

- The other thing that happens when nerves kick in is that the voice gets a tone higher. I am sure we have all witnessed a nervous talker rabbiting on in a higher than normal voice at what seems like 500 words a minute. As well as keeping it slow… keep it low!

- The conversation you are going to have should be just that, a conversation, and the last thing we want to do is argue. Standing your ground in a firm but professional and courteous manner is one thing, arguing with your boss is another. Never argue...always discuss!

- With the above in mind, should you find the conversation is indeed drifting into argue mode then the following statement, said in a passive, heartfelt and non-condescending manner will normally defuse the situation:

'Mr Jones, all I'm trying to do is have a conversation about this. I sincerely don't want to argue'.

I accept that on the page here, this statement may look a little wooden but again, it's all in the delivery, and with a little practice will ensure that IF the phrase is needed it can be delivered in a calm, confident and conciliatory way.

- Communication is a two-way thing. We <u>want</u> them to talk and discuss. So, when your boss is talking it's imperative that you listen. Listen and show you are listening and don't interrupt and don't assume. Hear your boss out, even if what they are saying is, in your view, an inaccurate version of how things really are. Remember…

'If You Want to be Heard….
Then Listen'

In general terms, the tone of voice is vital. It needs to be firm, natural but also purposeful. I am sure we have also all experienced when people have got the tone of voice wrong and how they meant something to come across actually comes across totally differently. With this in mind, we only have to look at that most wonderful of phrases 'I love you' to appreciate just how important tone of voice is.

Said slowly, with sincerity and with true heartfelt meaning, the phrase can leave us happy, elated, contented and in lots of cases, totally blissed out. The exact same three words, said as we hurriedly dash out of the door to work in the morning can sound simply a cliché and quite meaningless.

Tone of voice is vital, and it needs practice.

Our General Approach & Demeanour

Perhaps at this point it is worth reminding ourselves just what we are trying to do and achieve here.

The conversation we are going to have with our DB is not about scoring points and is not about 'winning' and it's not about being perceived as overly smart. However, it is about having a professional, polite and courteous conversation that will lead to all parties benefiting.

So, with this in mind, we need to adopt a general demeanour and attitude that displays this – and correct body language will help. We are not looking to 'win' but are looking to 'obtain agreement' – and while we do need to be strong and subtly assertive, displaying a respectful approach will help the wheels of communication turn.

On the respect front, yes, it is true that we might not like our DB too much and respect might indeed be something that is a long way off. However, they are, nevertheless the boss and for this they do deserve our respect, even though they might not have earned our unbridled love and devotion.

The bottom line? They are the boss and they have the power. You will not force them into anything and a general approach that is based around heartfelt but firm and well-prepared communication is the way forward.

So, we have the content worked out (including our Benefit Statement) and we have looked at how we are going to deliver it (our body language and our tone of voice) – and while we are not going to go into full blown rehearsals we will spend some quality time running through what we want to say and practicing!

The next thing to look at is timing. Just WHEN is the best time to have the conversation?

KEY MESSAGES:

- Think about and pay attention to your posture, your Body Language. Get this right and it will support and compliment the words you say.

- Practice! This conversation could turn out to be the best and most important of your year. It's worth practising it.

- The tone of voice should be calm, relaxed and authentic. Make it conciliatory and heartfelt.

- When your boss speaks listen. It's a two-way process.

Building Brick Four: Choosing the Moment

In the workplace, as in life itself, timing can be a crucial thing and if we can select the right moment to speak, then the chances of the conversation going our way are greatly increased. However, there is no blue print for saying that any particular moment is that magical 'right time' – and what appeared on paper to be the perfect time can turn out to be anything but. This said, there are certainly a few guidelines to help us select the best time. These come under two fundamental options.

OPTION ONE:

The prearranged meeting where an appointment is put in the diary.

OPTION TWO:

The 'pop-in' conversation where you observe your boss. You observe and sense they are in a receptive mood and so choose the moment 'in the moment' to have the conversation.

As you can see, it's a choice of two. Do you make an appointment to see your DB, or stay in a state of readiness waiting for the right moment when you think the conversation has a good chance of being well received?

Now, in some organisations, the boss is so busy and their life so scheduled that grabbing them at the right moment is simply not an option and so, in these instances, it will have to be an appointment

However, let's have a look at the pros and cons of both…

Option One: The Pre-arranged Meeting/Conversation

You decide to go for Option One. Your boss may or may not have a PA or secretary who organises their schedule, but if they do, then this may help matters as you will hopefully not get questioned too much about the purpose and reason for the meeting. If they do ask what the meeting is about simply say it's to discuss a few ideas you have about things in general. If they push again just say it's to discuss ideas and thoughts about improving efficiency.

If your boss does not have a PA, you will probably organise the meeting with them yourself. If this is done by e-mail this again may help things, but as above, if you have to inform them about the topic of the meeting then try and keep this as ambiguous as possible, perhaps using the two examples that have just been highlighted.

If, on the other hand, you have a face-to-face conversation to set up the meeting then this perhaps needs more careful attention.

Here's the scenario:

David is your boss. You go to David's office or work station and, after initial pleasantries, ask if you could book in a 15-minute chat – perhaps for the next day or a day that is right for you both.

The next big question that you need to be prepared for is what to say when David replies…

'Sure, let's meet at 3pm on Friday, but Shamela, what is it you want to talk to me about?'

In the perfect world, it would be better if this question was not asked and in the boss's mind the topic of the meeting is left blank, but it's not unreasonable for them to ask and in many ways they do have a right to know.

Now, the danger with their question is that if we give too much information to them then the conversation can almost start there and then and you can find yourself getting dragged into a discussion you didn't want to have at that particular moment (I often refer to this type of meeting as corridor or water cooler meetings).

Alternatively, if you don't reveal the topic of the meeting then we, at best, would be seen as being extremely mysterious, secretive and, at worst, downright uncooperative. Again, your boss probably does have a right to know ahead of the meeting just what the topic or subject to be discussed is, so be prepared for them to ask.

So, in this instance, a slight side step is the best approach and a reply of *'I've just got a few thoughts I'd like to discuss with you'* will hopefully fend them off. If pressed further, simply say *'I have a few thoughts on how we can perhaps improve things and I would like to discuss them'*.

This will normally work, but if <u>really</u> pressed simply say *'While I do have some thoughts about how to improve things and get more done, they are not totally formulated yet. David, can I talk you through it all properly on Friday at 3pm'*.

Said in the right way, with a tone of voice that says 'please play ball with me', this <u>WILL</u> do the trick.

So, if you do go for Option One, be prepared to be asked the question 'What do you want to see me about?' but more importantly, understand that while you don't want to say too much and so start the meeting there and then, you do have to give some indication to your boss.

Now, the downside of going for Option One is that with the meeting established for Friday at 3pm, the appointed hour comes along only for you to find your boss in a very stressed frame of mind and quite grumpy. However, you have committed to 3pm and you are almost forced to proceed – even though you know the timing has turned out to be terrible.

You can, however, alleviate the horror of finding your boss in one of his or her grumpy moods by stepping back and giving the 'picking the right time' challenge a little thought. Do this and you can be well on the way to choosing the right time.

If you know they are always in a dreadful mood after a weekly sales meeting, then that is not the right time to talk. If you know that Thursday morning, when they review the budgets, always leaves them with a migraine, then steer away from Thursdays. Perhaps Friday morning, prior to the weekly lunch with the MD might leave them tense and pre-occupied – but just possibly Friday afternoon might see them more relaxed, <u>especially</u> if you know that the forthcoming lunch meeting will probably go well as your boss had some good news to deliver to the MD.

Of course, all of the above are rather naive examples but they give you the idea that a little thought can really pay dividends.

Let's have a look at Option Two.

Option Two: The 'Hover' Conversation

Option Two is really about using your intuition. While this can sound very unscientific, you probably know your DB pretty well. You know their moods, what makes them happy and what makes them unhappy.

So, Option Two is really about what I call 'Hovering' – hovering and observing your boss so as to pick the moment when you think they are in a good and receptive mood.

This approach can have big benefits but it does have downsides to, one being that you need to be in a constant state of readiness at all times as you wait for that elusive right moment to appear. Now, of course this might take days – and if you are a little anxious about having the conversation in the first place then you can spend an entire week in a state of nervous frazzle. On the plus side, and it is a big plus, you are almost guaranteed to catch them at their best – when they are indeed in their most receptive mood.

Irrespective of which approach you take, one thing is definitely true, never talk to your DB about their behaviour, or indeed even request a meeting to discuss it if you are in any way angry, upset, annoyed, frustrated or generally wound up by how they have just treated you.

Yes, the desire to simply let them have both barrels immediately after they have been unreasonable can be strong, but the conversation where you turn your DB into a GB must be held when you are in a totally calm state of mind and when PREPERATION has taken place. Flying off the handle and demanding *'I need to talk to you right now'* is not the way forward.

The final thing to think about is interruptions. The conversation that you have with your DB is most certainly a very important one and if at all possible, you do not want to be interrupted. Some bosses will play into our hands by having a closed-door policy for all meetings and conversations – but others will not.

If you know that your boss is prone to allowing all and sundry into their office unannounced then you might need to give thought to this and pre-empt the problem by requesting that the door be closed and all calls go to voicemail for a few minutes. Often just making this request at the start of the conversation will send a message that you mean business and the conversation is an important one.

> ### KEY MESSAGES:
>
> - Timing is everything, so give it quality thought.
> - There are fundamentally two options, the pre-arranged meeting or the 'hover' approach.
> - Take time to pick the one that best suits you.

Building Brick Five:
Your Frame of Mind

So, this is where we are:

- Via a detailed analytical assessment, you know in your heart but more importantly in your head that your boss is indeed a DB and that it's not you.

- You also now appreciate that unless you take positive action, nothing will change and your Difficult Boss will remain just that... difficult!

- You have decided to take action. You have prepared well and your conversation will start with the all-important **Benefit Statement**.

- In addition, you have wisely kept your preparation and intentions confidential so there is no chance of your conversation being sabotaged by work place gossip.

- You understand and appreciate that deep down your DB is a reasonable person, though it's possible that pandering to their better nature simply may not work.

- You now appreciate and understand that when you actually have the conversation, your body language and tone of voice will be all important.

- In addition, we know that while we need to be strong in purpose, it will pay dividends if our general demeanour is respectful and courteous.

- You appreciate the importance of practice and understand that winging it on the day will not work.

- Lastly, you have given time and thought to selecting what you think will be the best possible moment to have the conversation and you are all ready to go for it!

So, against all this preparation, what is the one thing that can scupper your plans? ... The answer:

ANXIETY & NERVOUSNESS

It is a proven fact that anxiety and nervousness are the number one impeders of great performance of any sort and so we need to manage those two unwelcome intruders if we are going to deliver our message in the best possible way.

My Company, Brilliant Training Limited, delivers a lot of presentation skills training to organisations big and small across the UK and on these courses, a topic that is always high priority is *'How do I stop myself getting so nervous when I have to make a presentation?'* As a result of this we do a lot of work in what we call Anxiety Management.

So, if the prospect of actually having a conversation with your boss fills you with more than a few nerves, then you are in good hands. Worry not, because there are approaches and techniques you can adopt to significantly reduce these.

Of course, when you have the conversation with your DB it will not be a formal presentation – but in reality, it shouldn't be a million miles away. Just like a good presentation it will be pre-planned, correctly structured and, of course, practiced. However, as with a presentation, there is also a good chance that it will contain a degree of anxiety and nervousness too, unless of course we take positive action to manage these nerves!

So, yes, it's natural to have at least a few butterflies in the tummy before any important conversation – but let's make sure we have them flying in tight formation!

So just how do we get those butterflies to fly how we want? Here are a few tips:

Managing 'The Voices' (Internal Dialogue)

Lightening Tony Jones is an aspiring heavyweight championship boxer. He is skilful and talented and people in the know say he has a great future. To date, he has had eight fights and has convincingly won them all. However, tonight he faces Steve 'Giant' Brown – a huge man, who although past his prime, has had his moments during his long career.

All of the pundits, however, realise that Lightening Tony has all the skills to overcome his bigger slower opponent. All he has to do is stay calm, deploy the right tactics and have belief in himself.

However, the big moment arrives and Lightening Tony enters the ring and looks across at Giant Brown. At this point Lightning's thoughts go something like this…

> *'Oh my God – he is massive! He is a man mountain. I knew he was big but not this huge. If he hits me with a good punch, I don't think I will survive. He is a giant.'*

Lightening Tony takes a seat on the stool in the corner of the ring and as the MC announces each boxer, the following runs through Tony's mind…

> *'This is just too big a step up for me. I'm not ready for this yet. I may be quick but if he gets one good punch on me, I'm done. Also, when I do hit him, he will hardly feel it and*

I'm hardly going to knock him out. This fight is a big mistake.
I'm not ready for this and it's too big a challenge'.

QUESTION?

Despite Lightening Tony Jones being talented, well prepared and with a great future ahead of him, what now are his chances of success?

The answer, of course, is a lot slimmer than before he saw Giant Brown and before he started to have all the negative thoughts, for while Tony has all of the attributes needed to go out and win, he is, in effect, sabotaging his chances by having the wrong kind of thoughts – the wrong kind of Internal Dialogue.

Now, fortunately, few of us have to face the physical pressure situation that Lightening Tony had to face but let me ask you a question, have you yourself ever been faced with a pressure situation of your own, one that you were none too keen to undertake and found that you had negative voices in the head rather like Tony?

The reality is that we don't have to be a boxer to face challenges that we are none too keen to take on and they can come along at frequent intervals. Ranging from an interview for a big job to a best man's speech, a visit to the dentist to asking out an admired member of the opposite sex – they can all cause us anxiety and nervousness.

So, as the big moment looms and we are approaching the day or time when we will talk to our DB then, for a lot of people, the thoughts start, but sadly in 99% of cases they are not very positive or helpful ones!

Of course, internal dialogue is a very personal thing that is unique to each individual but here are a few examples of the more common negative voices that can roam around our heads:

'I know this won't work; I don't know why I am even trying.'

'I know people will see how nervous I am.'

'Why did I ever agree to this; I know it will be a disaster.'

'She/he will never go out with someone like me; why even ask!'

'I know he won't change; what's the point in even asking.'

'Things never go how I want them to.'

'I know they won't give a job like that to me, so why even apply?'

As you can see, all of the above have one thing in common, they are all VERY negative and as such, they do nothing at all to help our performance. However, it's not just the case that they don't help us, they actually dramatically hinder us. For all of the research confirms that negative internal dialogue is very destructive and it can sabotage our best laid plans, ruin our aspirations and generally do immeasurable damage.

So, what is the answer?

Well, the answer is, in effect, incredibly simple, though at times so simple people discount it – even though it is backed up by endless scientific and medical research that PROVES that it works.

In simple terms, all we have to do to start the process of having a super confident mind-set is to replace the negative thoughts – thoughts that will destroy our chances – with super positive ones.

Of course, this can appear to be a pretty big challenge if we are indeed feeling very nervous and so negative about the coming challenge, but one of the key reasons why we do feel so negative is the very fact that we have such negative thoughts. In brief, we tell ourselves it's going to go very badly and so, understandably, we become nervous about the forthcoming failure. What we need to do is change the thinking.

You see, the fantastic thing about replacing negative thoughts with positive ones is that in the first instance, they do not have to be fact and you do not even have to believe them, you just have to 'believe' that you do.

This, I admit, is a strange concept to take on board but it is proven that the mind cannot distinguish between what is truth and what is fiction, and so by simply repeating key statements over and over again we in effect take them on board, take ownership of them and <u>make them reality</u>.

To drive home this proven concept, here are a few famous statements. Some are from people who knew a little about success as well as the role of positive thoughts in its attainment. All carry the same fundamental message:

> 'If you fail to control your own mind, you may be
> sure you will control nothing else'.
>
> Napoleon Hill

> 'Fear is only as deep as the mind allows'.
>
> Japanese proverb

> 'If you keep saying things are going to be bad, you
> have a good chance of becoming a prophet'.
>
> Isaac Singer

> 'Nothing on earth can stop the individual with the
> right mental attitude from achieving their goals –
> nothing on earth can help the individual with the
> wrong mental attitude'.
>
> WW Ziege

'Whether you think you can or you think you can't, you are right'.

Henry Ford

'We either make ourselves miserable and weak or we make ourselves happy and strong. The amount of effort is about the same'.

Carlos Castaneda

'Your altitude is controlled by your attitude'

Zig Ziglar

'Our imagination creates our reality'.

Tony Robbins

Still not convinced?

Well there is some amazing research highlighted in the book *Psycho Cybernetics* by Doctor Maxwell Maltz that gives an insight into the effects of mental preparation and visualisation – using basketball as the way to prove it works.

In the test, three groups of men were formed and identified as Groups A, B and C. Group A actually met every day and practiced what is called a free shot on a basketball court (a free shot is something akin to a penalty in football). They practiced every day for twenty days and their results were measured on day one and day twenty.

Group B were also scored on day one and day twenty, but engaged in no practice at all in between.

Group C were also measured on day one – but they met for the next eighteen days for just twenty minutes a day. When they met, they were sat in a circle and, one by one, they were asked to vividly imagine throwing the ball into the basket. When they imagined they had missed, they were asked to re-imagine, correcting their aim and throwing again and scoring.

On day twenty, the three groups all reconvened on the basketball court and all took the same amount of test shots at the basket. The results were, of course, recorded.

The results were as follows:

- Group A, who had practiced every day improved by 24%.

- Group B, who had done no practice at all showed no improvement.

- Group C, the group who practiced in their imagination improved by 23% ...yet they had not touched a basketball nor had they been on a basketball court.

This is the power of your mind and the power of your imagination!

The bottom line is that if, ahead of your conversation with you DB, you allow yourself to have negative thoughts and negative internal dialogue then you are seriously sabotaging and hindering your chances of success. On the other hand, if, like the men in Group C, you vividly imagine it going well then this will dramatically enhance your chances of it doing just that!

So what is the way forward?

Well, of course, it's quite simple. As we approach the conversation with our DB, we simply **DO NOT** allow ourselves the choice of feeding our mind with negative thoughts that simply reinforce our anxiety and make us fearful. Instead, we ditch the *Mind Garbage* and replace it with good healthy *Mind Food* – positive messages that are going to help us.

These, of course, need to be unique to you and your personality, but as the meeting with your DB approaches, and you feel the first tremors of anxiety, these are the sort of positive thoughts you need to be having…

- I am well prepared and this **WILL** go well.

- I am calm and in control – my butterflies are in formation.

- I refuse to let anxiety hinder me – I am super confident and relaxed.

- I **WILL** rise to this challenge – I **WILL** have this conversation.

- In my heart I **KNOW** it will go well.

- I am confident and calm.

- I need to have the conversation. It is my right and it **WILL** go well.

- I am calm, confident and well-practiced. This is going to work.

To anyone unfamiliar with this technique, I admit it may seem strange and even bizarre, but talk to any top competitive sportsman and they will tell you it works.

Again, I have to stress that your positive messages may indeed be the exact opposite to how you are actually feeling – but say them anyway and say them with conviction. Say them with belief. Say them with passion. Say them with commitment. Say them with unshakable certainty and BELIEVE! – because after all – where will thoughts like the ones Lightening Tony had get you?

You have a God-given right to have this conversation with your boss and **NOTHING** is going to stop you delivering it to the very best of your ability. Choose super positive thoughts as opposed to mind garbage and change your life!

The choice is yours… make the right choice!

The Power of Framing

Another technique that can be applied to help combat anxiety and nervousness is something called Framing.

Framing is about taking a situation or challenge that we are not looking forward to and framing it, or comparing it against an external situation that other people may be facing, something that is, in effect, far bigger and more daunting than the challenge that is causing us the anxiety. The objective here is to compare our situation against another and so see your worrisome situation in its true light.

Now, to make Framing work you have to delve into some powerful but often uncomfortable and even distressing scenarios. This is essential to bring the power of framing to life. Here is an example that I personally use – and I make no apology for its emotive nature.

When I am faced with a problem or a challenging and difficult day that is causing me anxiety, I consider this sobering thought:

> On average, on any given morning in the UK, four people tragically die as a result of traffic accidents. As a consequence, sometime during that particular day a member of their family – a loving wife, husband, mother, father or sibling gets a knock on the door and they are told the dreadful news. Their world, understandably, collapses.

Having just talked of having positive thoughts this scenario is, of course, utterly depressing. However, for a brief moment pause and consider how the recipient of such dreadful news must feel.

For the partner or relative, child or friend who learns of this news, it is a day of utter grief. The challenge of dealing with it is of indescribable proportions. Their discomfort, pain and agony are immense and almost unimaginable.

Compared with this dreadful situation, suddenly my particular challenge seems pretty insignificant and small!

Now, I don't want to devalue the anxiety and nervousness that you may be going through as the meeting and conversation that you are going to have with your DB approaches. The conversation is an important one and your DB is a difficult person to deal with and so it is natural that nervousness anxiety and even fear might take hold. However, what will help us get the challenge in proportion is to <u>Frame It</u> against something else.

So, when I am faced with a pressure situation, and being a public speaker and a trainer, I often am, I frame my particular challenge against something that is TRULY challenging.

Every day people are told they have incurable illnesses. Everyday brave peace keepers put their very existence on the line in war-torn countries. Firemen and Firewomen, lifeboat crews and the police all risk serious injury and even death dealing with truly horrible situations. Every day, people heroically face real fear and trauma and come through.

Compared to these, the challenge of having a conversation with our boss seems pretty small don't you agree?

Framing works but you need to make it emotive. Binning the negative voice in your head and replacing it with a positive voice also works, but you need to muster up the determination and desire to actually implement these proven techniques.

It is true that most people experience anxiety, nervousness and fear when faced with a difficult challenge but we most definitely have a choice about how we deal with them. We can either let them consume us – and so wreck or hopes and dreams and often our life, or we can get focused, get determined and even get angry, so much so that we think 'ENOUGH...I will not let this paralysis take control'.

Once again, the choice is yours – I implore you to make the right one!

> *'The Most Important Conversation You Will Have*
> *on Any Given Day is the One You Have with*
> *Yourself, So Make Sure It's a Good One'*
>
> Zig Ziglar

KEY MESSAGES:

- If unchecked, nerves and anxiety will seriously hinder the quality of the conversation we have with our boss.

- We have to manage the negative thoughts...our internal dialogue.

- We must replace negative thoughts with positive ones, even if initially we don't believe them.

- We can't take a magic pill to get rid of our nerves, but we can take something. It's called ACTION!

So that concludes this chapter, the biggest chapter in the book and chapter that explains the Five Building Bricks. The Five Bricks are...

1. Confidentiality

2. Preparation & Content

3. Delivery

4. Choosing the Moment

5. Your Attitude & Frame of Mind

Each one is important and each one needs to be applied methodically and with purpose.

The success of your particular conversation – and so your new improved relationship with your boss is built on the five Building Bricks.

8
The Full Conversation –
The 4 Key Steps

As we move towards the end of our journey, the final thing to do is to go back to the actual conversation with your DB and look at a few tips and pointers to help you continue the conversation to its positive conclusion.

As the author of this book, it is, of course, impossible to cover every angle on every conversation that is going to take place as a result of people reading this book – so the information that follows is intended as general assistance.

As you will see, the conversation with your boss is fundamentally made up of Four Steps. These are:

Step One: Deliver Your Benefit Statement

Step Two: Make Them 'Not Wrong'

Step Three: The Offer

Step Four: The Truth Statement:

Follow these in a literal step-by-step way and it will ensure your conversation has both a clear structure and tracks on which to run.

As far as the actual words are concerned, they are most definitely only there as an example of what a well-structured conversation might look like. They should not be learnt word for word as your particular conversation will be unique to you and your boss and will have a degree of free flow to it. However, of course, if there are any key phrases that you like then adopt and adapt them accordingly.

The other thing to say is that as you read the words on the page they may well come across as very wooden, very scripted and even a little crass – but yet again, it is all about the delivery (tone of voice etc). They exist to help guide you as you plan and practice your own conversation in your own style.

With practice in mind please don't get too hung up or concerned if each time you run through it you find it is slightly different, as to some degree it should be. Your conversation with your DB is just that, a conversation and you are not learning Hamlet or Macbeth. Yes, via practice become very comfortable with your Benefit Statement, but the objective is to 'converse' with your boss in a way that is natural and authentic to you.

So, the key is to get the key headings firmly planted in your head (i.e. the Step One to Step Two to Step Three to Step Four approach). Get these key milestones in place and the practise will ensure that when you do have the actual conversation it will flow naturally, but, more importantly, it **will** follow a designated path and you won't wander off track.

Here is a sample of what a full conversation might look like. You are going to have 'the' conversation with your boss, Helen.

You enter Helen's office and there is the normal exchange of pleasantries. With this in mind, a few seconds (or even a couple of minutes) of informal chit chat is normally not a bad thing – especially if Helen is in a friendly and engaging mood. However, if she is the type of DB who would never do this then be prepared to get straight into it.

So, one way or another Helen says… *'So, what can I do for you?'* At this point your perfectly structured and well-practiced conversation kicks in.

STEP ONE: START WITH THE BENEFIT STATEMENT;

You

'Helen thanks for seeing me. I have been having a think about things and about how I could be more productive around here. If there was a way, a method, that my general efficiency improved and I even made fewer of those errors that I'm sometimes prone to – well I wonder if that would be of interest?'

Having delivered the Benefit Statement, allow your boss to respond. The Benefit Statement is designed to get a 'Yes' answer. Be ready as this could come back at you very quickly.

Helen:

'Well yes of course. What are you suggesting? What do you mean?'

STEP TWO: MAKE THEM NOT WRONG:

Now, the last thing we want to do is immediately make your DB feel they are being criticised and attacked and we want to keep the doors of communication open. Therefore, what is needed is a short statement that subtly says to them *'Boss…I understand your position…I can see your point of view…however'*. Of course, the right demeanour and tone of voice are essential for achieving this. Remember, the way forward is to be conciliatory and not confrontational. As an example, you might want to try:

You

'I, of course, understand you are busy and always have a lot on and so I can only imagine the pressures and demands that go with the job...'

STEP THREE: MAKE YOUR OFFER:

Having in your own words said something similar to this continue with...

You

'However, if I am totally honest, I know you're not getting the best out of me and I could and want to deliver more for you.'

Now at this point, it's fair to say the average Helen, while interested, is probably not going to simply fall at your feet. She may well be a little cautious about where the conversation is going and it may indeed feel to her like she is being criticised.

As stated, normally bosses don't like being criticised, especially by people who work for them so perhaps it might be necessary to take the sting out of things. You might want to try the following:

You

'I do appreciate you want things done in a certain way and I do want to deliver the best quality of work that I can.'

To which Helen might say: *'OK, what do you mean?*

STEP FOUR: DELIVER THE TRUTH STATEMENT
(BE BRAVE … STICK TO YOUR GUNS)

Remember, nothing will change unless you change it and to bring about the change we need and deserve we need to let our DB see the truth. So, gather your courage and calmly and professionally deliver the Truth Statement, the statement or statements that let your DB know they could get so much more out of you.

But what is a Truth Statement?

Well first of all it's part of the conversation that, rather like your Benefit Statement, needs to be thought about, constructed and indeed practiced **before** you have the conversation with your DB. As to what it is … well it's a statement, or at least key part of the overall conversation, that very honestly lets your DB know that firstly they could get a more out of you, and secondly that the way they are currently managing you IS causing you discomfort, unhappiness and even pain.

As an example, the Truth Statement like look like this:

You

'Helen, if I can be totally honest you would get more out of me if I was perhaps managed a little differently.'

Helen

'What do you mean?

Dig deep and continue with a Truth Statement:

You

'I appreciate that some people work well by being managed in a robust style but if I am really honest, I am not one of them. I know I make the odd mistake and I admit possibly too many – but if I wasn't always living in a state of anxiety and fear I know I would deliver SO much more for you.

'Helen, I do understand the big responsibilities you have and I know you have to ultimately get the job done but the sarcasm, excessive critical comments and at times, occasional choice language does nothing for me and it generally saps my confidence and makes me feel dreadful.

'Helen, this is not easy. I'm not looking for special treatment, I'm just trying to be honest and move things forward so I do a better job for you.'

Of course, on the printed page, all of the above might appear as if it's from some fairy tale world where everything goes just right. I also accept that they may come across as overly scripted. However, delivered in a conversational and heartfelt manner will ensure that the Four Stage approach as set out above WILL work.

It will work because the tone of voice is conciliatory and non-judgemental, but more importantly, it will work because the conversation has some subtle but very strong messages – and such statements as 'I know I would deliver SO much more **for you**' and 'I'm just trying to be honest and move things forward so I do a better job **for you**' are all very compelling from a boss's point of view!

Here are the key stages of the conversation again:

Step One: Deliver Your Benefit Statement
                This gets their attention and interest.

Step Two: **Make Them 'Not Wrong'**
                 Conciliatory words that say 'I understand your
                 position'.

Step Three: **The Offer**
                 Informs them they could get more efficiency and
                 productivity from you.

Step Four: **The Truth Statement:**
                 Indicates to them what they need to do/not do to
                 get more from you.

Once the fourth step has been delivered, it is really over to your boss for their responses and thoughts. At this point, it is very important to both listen and stay very focused. From here the conversation will take a path that is unique to you and your boss and so, as you can appreciate, it is simply not possible to legislate for your particular conversation once past the Four Steps. However, the Four Step Approach will have definitely set the conversation off on the right path.

So, as the conversation continues, remain calm and keep the good body language and tone of voice. Remember, it's a friendly conversation. It's not an argument and it's not aggressive…It has a benefit for both parties at its core.

With the ongoing conversation in mind, here are some additional tips.

- Keep in mind that even the most onerous boss will struggle when they are faced with the fact that they do truly hinder and even hurt people with their management style. Yes, there are bosses out there who seem to think that dishing out sarcastic and even overtly critical comments is almost a sport, but that is because they truly have no idea just how hurtful their approach is. You may be surprised to know that, confronted with the reality of the situation, many aggressive DB's are mortified to discover the true effect of their management style.

- With the above in mind, do not be afraid to say quite clearly that their style and manner does indeed hurt. Letting your DB know your true feelings can be very powerful. True and sincere honesty works and can never be wrong.

- If your DB is the kind that is ultra-sparing with praise, the following might help:

'Mr Clarke, I appreciate praise has to be earned – but I do respond to praise and you would get more out of me if I was acknowledged more.'

- For increased potency (and with a little practice), try adding a Benefit Statement onto the end of a Truth Statement…

'David, if I can be really honest, ridiculing me in front of colleagues makes me feel dreadful (Truth Statement). *You would get so much more out of me if these instances didn't occur' (Benefit Statement).*

If you are concerned that things might start to go astray and that your DB might become impatient, agitated or even mildly annoyed then the following statements – delivered with true sincerity – will normally work (you will see all finish with a Benefit Statement…with something for them).

'Mrs Peters, all I am trying to do here is improve things and deliver more for you.'

'Helen, I am not wishing to argue here...all I want to do is improve things and so deliver better work for you.'

'Mr Jones, it's not my intention to fall out...all I wanted to do was talk to you honestly about how I can work more effectively and efficiently for you.'

What to Expect:

So, as the conversation concludes what happens?

We know that every boss is different and so it's impossible to say just how your particular boss will respond. However, generally there are just two types of responses, and the first one is very good news!

I know that earlier in this book we said that appealing to your boss's better nature was perhaps a lost cause and certainly, in some cases if they are high on the Difficult Scale, this is true. However, with a DB who is a little less onerous, the realisation that they have been causing you genuine discomfort and even pain can be a big moment for them. If this is the case, as it often is, they can definitely fall into the first type of response as set out below.

ONE: THE INSTANT RESPONSE

Here is the good news! In a lot of cases, we find that once the boss has been made fully aware of the negative impact they are having, they are genuinely surprised, shocked and even mortified. Yes, they may have been aware that they had a 'robust' management style but often they have been oblivious to its negative and even destructive impact. As a result, they feel true regret, to the point where an apology can often be forthcoming.

I appreciate that if your DB is particularly challenging and mid to high on the scale, you may feel that this is an unlikely outcome, but it can certainly happen (this is definitely the case if they are the kind of boss who is normally a little short on emotional intelligence).

Alternatively, if they are the type of boss who gets so focused and absorbed in trying to get the job done that they lose sight of the emotional impact their constant pushing has had, then again your revelations may truly get through to them.

In brief, you have brought to their attention just how rotten they make you feel and this has immediately resonated with them. They are surprised, shocked and even remorseful that they have caused you pain. Your conversation has definitely worked and it's had an immediate and visible effect.

TWO THE DELAYED RESPONSE

A delayed response usually comes from a DB who is, to some degree, aware that they can be a little unreasonable and even perhaps aggressive at times, but in their world they justify this with thoughts based around *'I'm just trying to get the job done'* and *'I'm not here to be popular'*.

With this type of DB, it's fair to say you probably won't get an immediate positive response, but that's **not** to say your conversation has failed.

Often this type of boss needs time to process things, to reflect and to think things through. So, while it is the case that you may not get an immediate 'I'm sorry', what tends to happen is that over the following few days the things you have said start to seep through and they do start to realise that changing would be a good idea.

The key message here: don't be put off if, initially, your feel your conversation has not been well received. With a lot of bosses, they just need time to process things.

KEY MESSAGES:

- The conversation needs to have a defined structure and shape so it does not ramble and go off track.

- Following the Four Step principle will help this happen.

- With the fourth step delivered, allow the conversation to develop naturally.

- Expect one of two responses from your boss.

9
A Few Final Thoughts
(A Few Final Doubts?)

So, apart from the three Bonus Chapters that follow, our journey is almost over.

As we reach the end of our voyage, I hope that the information contained in this Brilliant Little Book has been of use and I hope it has fired up some real energy for change. However, I also appreciate that as we come to a close there may be a few people out there who, while having taken on board all of the tips and techniques contained, still have a fundamental nagging fear about implementing the process of Managing Up.

If you are in this camp, perhaps the thoughts below might strike a chord?

'Yes – but what happens if it all goes wrong?'

'What happens if I try and nothing happens?'

'What happens if it all backfires and it makes things worse?'

Well, in principle, all are possible – but if you are thinking any of the above, here are two important things to think about.

ONE:

It is true that despite a well prepared and professionally executed delivery, your boss might still not engage in the process of change. However, in most instances, if they are followed correctly, the tips, techniques, attitudes and strategies contained in the book **will** help you create a **major** force for the positive change you seek.

TWO:

More importantly, in respect of the whole process backfiring and it making things worse, you are probably not alone on this one and it's a very common doubt to have, but it's crucially important to remember this…

If you follow the procedure and advice set out in this book, you will, by definition, have asked the question 'Is It Me… Am I the Cause of my Boss's Bad Behaviour?' Having posed and answered the question, and found yourself in Group B or C, you will then have done the following:

- Made a real attempt to understand your boss, to understand their pressures and their challenges. You will also have acknowledged that despite their unwelcome management style, they ARE human.

- Maintained confidentiality at all times, eliminating any careless and unprofessional gossip that could scupper your chances.

- Prepared your conversation correctly and included a Benefit Statement. You appreciate there has to be something in it for the boss.

- You have practised and run through what you will say.

- You have picked the right moment when you feel your boss will be in a conducive mood for listening.

- You have used good tone of voice and good body language. While assertive, your general demeanour has been non-confrontational.

- You have 'discussed and not argued'.

- You have harnessed any anxiety and nervousness via framing and creating positive internal dialogue.

- You have not tried to 'score points' or 'win' – but have acted throughout in a totally professional, polite, confidential and courteous manner.

So, against this background, is it not true that it would be extremely difficult – if not impossible – for your boss to take offence at or umbrage with your actions?

Remember, the process you are going through, the process of Managing Up is NOT wrong. It is not a criminal offence nor is it against company policy – and if you do it correctly in the aforementioned professional, confidential and courteous manner then it's VERY difficult, if not impossible, for it to be held against you!

Of course, ultimately the question 'To Speak Up or Not Speak Up' has to be your individual decision but I hope that the contents of this book have given you some additional tools to help you make your decision a positive one. I also hope these last few pointers about any final doubts have helped – for remember, if you do nothing, then nothing is ever likely to change.

If you do, on the other hand, engage in the process of Managing Up, but still your boss regrettably refuses to engage in change then at least you have the inner satisfaction of knowing you can say '*At least I had the courage to try!*' This feeling alone can do wonders for the inner you.

So, remember, Managing Up can seriously change your life! Here are a few last thoughts:

- Managing Up can indeed seriously change your life for the better, and if implemented correctly, it can also be a real force for good for your company too.

- This book is NOT anti-boss. Bosses do a very difficult job and often in very demanding circumstances. Bosses are essential for the success of any organisation and I wholeheartedly support their existence.

- When implementing the Managing Up process, don't expect an immediate change to occur. Your boss might come around slowly. They might need time to ponder and come to terms with things. So, don't expect them to come to work the next day dressed in a superman suit, knickers over their trousers or skirt and with **Super Boss** written on their chest! It can take time!

- To Talk or Not to Talk is your decision and it can feel a big decision – but it is highly likely that nothing will change unless you change it.

- You have a right as a professional and as a member of the human race to take action. Make that action confidential, professional and courteous and it will be difficult if not impossible to be criticised for it.

- Make your conversation honest and heartfelt – but ensure it contains a Benefit Statement.

- Prepare well and practice.

So, apart from the final two bonus chapters, we reach the end. The last thing I have to do is make a sincere and humble apology to all readers whose boss IS actually called Mr Jones, Helen or any of the other names we have used. By now I'm sure we are all a little tired of them – but to those who have a real Mr Jones or a Helen in their life...well to you I specifically apologise!

So now it's over to you. Are you ready to step up and Manage Up – or suffer at the hands of a difficult boss for who knows how long? – for remember this...

To suffer at the hands of a difficult boss can be a very traumatic experience.

To summon up the courage to take action can be incredibly empowering.

To see the results of your courage can be life changing!

Over To You. Take Action. Take Ownership.

Manage Up

BONUS CHAPTER 1

Something for the Bosses:

Many years ago, when I was a young thrusting and slightly power mad Regional Manager in the world of retailing, I had to carry out the yearly appraisals for the Managers of my 15 stores.

The first 14 went pretty well, or so I thought, and when I got to the final section of each conversation I asked the following question:

> 'So, Ms Manager...is there anything that I can do,
> or need to be doing to improve my performance in
> order to help you more.'

On the first fourteen occasions, I received a respectful and at times cooing:

> 'Oh no, Mr Lewis, everything is just fine, thank you.'

I continued about my business in a happy state of ignorant euphoria. My world, was about to change!

My mother always said *'Watch out for the quiet ones, they can be trouble'* and manager Number 15 was, I guess, just that. I will call her Ann and she was about 28, tiny in stature and quiet in demeanour, but, as I was about to discover, she had a rod of steel down her spine.

The appraisal took place on a Friday. It had all gone to plan and so as I asked my now well used last question I was already packing my briefcase to go. However, Ann was reading from a different script and, unlike her previous 14 contemporaries, she most definitely had something to say.

In a quiet but noticeably determined tone Ann responded thus:

> *'Well actually, Mr Lewis, there is...in fact there are*
> *quite a few things... In fact, I have made a list.'*

As I said, I was slightly full of my own importance, so as Ann proceeded to rattle off a list of my misdemeanours my first thought was something along the lines of *'How dare you criticise me … you're finished'* – a thought which, I admit, I quickly became very ashamed of. Fortunately, the thing that saved the appraisal from turning into World War Three was that I had to go to a store an hour away to carry out some interviews.

So, trying to contain my seething anger, I calmly asked Ann if we could park the contents of her 'very important list' until Monday when I would return to give it my full attention – though I admit my actual thought at the time was more like *'When I come back to sack you'* (this was not something I could or would have done, but I admit it's how I felt at the time).

During the journey to the next store, I was seething and you could have run my car on the power of my anger. As I conducted the interviews that afternoon my main objective had become to find not one manager but two, this so that I could replace Ann! By the evening, entrenched in my hotel, I was starting to calm down. By the next morning, I started to see things differently and by the evening, when I finally got back to my home and my wife, I was almost suicidal!

For, during the subsequent 30 or so hours from my meeting with Ann, I had in my mind run through her list of failings – and once my arrogant pride had subsided, I realised that every single one of them was 100% true.

I was not 'Mr Fantastic' – the man who was on the top of his game – but more, an uncaring, un-noticing and un-focused young upstart who failed to realise that great management and great leadership has listening, giving and supporting at its heart. In brief, quiet unassuming Ann changed my career and indeed changed my life. I started to see that management and leadership was about 'them' and not 'me'.

In my defence, I was not a bully and was not cruel, but I was very focused on me and on any given day, it was 'my' agenda that always took preference, with theirs tagged on at the end, if I had time.

So that's my story! It might strike a chord and it might not. But, having read this chapter, and if you are indeed a boss, then you may be curious to find out where you stand in the league of excellence. Are you a GB (Good Boss) or a DB (Difficult Boss)?

Of course, there are many requirements to being a great manager and a great boss and not all are related to the people management side of things, but one thing that I have learnt over the years is this... get the team motivated, happy and inspired – and pretty much everything else falls into place.

So, are your team members, be they one or one hundred, motivated, happy and inspired? More importantly do you really know if they are or not? How much quality time do you commit to them? Do you know what truly makes them tick? Do you know their aspirations and dreams? Are you helping them with these? Are you helping them grow?

Do you truly motivate them? Do you inspire them? Do you know specifically how to get the best out of them? Have you asked them this question? Do you know what they are afraid of? Do you train them? Do you really commit to them? Do you care?

Being a boss is a tough, tough job and you only find out how tough when you get there. However, having a team behind you who are committed and enthusiastic and inspired makes all the difference, and if you doubt that, simply transfer the concept to sport. Would the Barcelona football team or the mighty All Blacks rugby team have been so successful if they had not had commitment and enthusiasm at their heart?

For the million-dollar question is this:

> *Does your team, be it a team of one or one*
> *hundred, run on commitment or compliance?*

Do they carry out each task because they **want** to or because they **have** to? If its compliance your team is running on half power. If its commitment, you are on the path to glory and achieving YOUR full potential – because one thing is certain, you yourself will never achieve your full potential unless your team does.

So, if you're a GB then may I offer you sincere congratulations – as you will truly understand that amazing feeling of knowing you are an inspiring and empowering force and that you make people 'more'. If, on the other hand, you think you might be veering towards the DB side of things then think this, 'What a great opportunity I have to bring about REAL positive improvement'.

Nothing more to add! Thanks for reading this section 'Something for the Bosses'. If you want to find out more about how to truly be an exceptional boss who really gets the best out of a team, have a look at The Brilliant Little Book **How To Be A Brilliant Boss**. It's full of everything you need to know to TRULY inspire, motivate and lead.

BONUS CHAPTER 2

Managing Up…& The Boss Who Is Not Too Bad

This Bonus Chapter is really for the people out there who only occasionally struggle with their boss, and whose boss is really not too bad at all.

By and large he or she is a petty reasonable human being but, for whatever the reason, at certain times can still act in a way that causes you frustration, anguish and even mild pain.

Now this type of boss perhaps does not qualify to carry the full title of DB – but does however sometimes drift into areas of behaviour that have a negative effect on either your work & general performance, your mood & well-being – or both!

By definition this type of boss sits quite low on the Difficult Chart and comes in somewhere between 1 and 3. However, that's not to say that the relationship cannot be improved!

The good news is that taking action to mutually improve the relationship is really very easy and it does not require the detailed and highly structured approach that is needed when dealing with a full-blown DB. For while dealing with a DB who is high on the Difficult Chart needs a very precise approach it's fair to say that when trying to improve things with a boss who is 'not too bad' then all that is needed is often nothing more than a 'friendly chat'.

Here are a few tips and approaches that you may want to think about and implement:

- The first thing to understand is that just like when dealing with a full-blown DB some form of conversation will be needed. By and large the relationship you have with your boss is ok, but if you feel it could be better than this improvement won't happen by magic. A conversation will be needed.

- Before you do this take time to step back and analysis the situation in detail. Firstly, you do of course have to ensure that you are keeping your side of the bargain and you are in group B or group C, this as set out back on pages 35 and 36

- Next, give some thought to just why they do the things that annoy or upset you – i.e. what is driving their behaviour? If most of the time they are indeed a pretty reasonable person are they doing it unknowingly? – or alternatively are they aware they are at times a little challenging, annoying or thoughtless – but not really aware of the negative impact this has on you? Is it when they themselves are under pressure then their emotional intelligence and their mood radar inadvertently gets switched off?

- Consider this pretty big question: With you feeling and believing that they are basically a reasonable human being are you confident that if you have the right type of conversation with them, then there IS a 'better nature' lurking within them that you can appeal to (needless to say if you think not, then you may want to reconsider your approach),

- The conversation you are going to have with them will be based around the 'friendly chat' approach. However, that is not to say that you can be complacent at all. So, with this in mind having a look at the Five Building Bricks before you decide to move forward may well be a good idea. In brief, making sure we have things like Confidentiality, Preparation & Practice, your Body Language, your Tone of Voice and lastly your Attitude all fully engaged is still a good idea.

- The whole basis of a conversation with a full-blown DB is that we understand the conversation has to have something in it for them. However, the conversation with the boss who is generally ok is based on appealing to their better nature. But this is not to say that starting the whole conversation off with a Benefit Statement is not a bad idea! (So take the time to prepare a good one).

- After starting with a Benefit Statement let the conversation develop naturally. However, you perhaps do still need to include some form of Truth Statement that says to your boss that sometimes, on occasions, they do make me feel less than good (unless we let them know they do cause frustration/pain etc they probably won't realise they need to change).

- Finally, as the conversation progresses don't be surprised if your boss is genuinely surprised and even shocked to discover that they have on occasions been causing you frustration, distress and even pain. They are after all a reasonable person – and no reasonable person likes to unwittingly hurt another human being.

In conclusion, managing a boss who is not too onerous at all is itself not too difficult – but it does need a conversation and they will not change by magic. However, the conversation can be friendly and even chatty by nature, but it does still need to contain a degree of structure – this to ensure your message is delivered correctly.

BONUS CHAPTER 3

General Tips to Help the Workplace Relationship

Talk in Boss Language:

Communicating with your boss in a style and manner that they like will, of course, help the relationship. So, if your boss likes a weekly summary then, of course, this is the way forward. If, on the other hand they like daily e-mails to keep them updated then the daily e-mail it is. Also, generally, do they like information in headlines or are they a detail person? Whatever way they like to communicate if you can work it out and then talk in their particular 'boss language', it will definitely help the relationship.

Take Along the Problem – But Take a Solution Too:

I know from personal experience that when a member of the team comes and informs you of a problem and then says something along the lines of *'So what should I do?'*…well let's just say it can get slightly annoying!

What really works is to certainly make the boss aware of the challenge, but then to suggest one or two solutions or ideas that you have had to remedy things. Something along the lines of:

> *'Helen, I need to let you know that the binding machine has broke so, we are struggling to get the reports ready for your board meeting. I thought we could either send*

> *them out to our stationary suppliers who can do it for us*
> *or I could try and talk to the Accounts Department, who I*
> *think also have a binder.'*

Taking along a solution with every problem will really endear you to your boss. Yes, it is not guaranteed they will buy into your solutions but at least you have tried to be proactive and helpful.

Don't Give Them Nasty Shocks:

Of course, no one wants to be the bearer of bad news and telling a boss who is perhaps prone to flying off the handle can be a little daunting. As a result, it's understandable that the *'I'll tell them tomorrow'* paralysis can creep in. This approach can be compounded when it's joined by the *'Let's see if it sorts itself out… they may not even need to know'* style of thinking.

It is true that sometimes, though not too often, things can miraculously fix themselves. However, is it not the case that usually a problem that is not dealt with just festers and gets worse?

From a boss's perspective, and again I speak from experience, the worst thing that can happen is that you think everything is going along quite nicely when out of the blue a bombshell lands. This can be bad enough but when you discover that the problem has been around for a while, but no one told you, it can make the blood boil.

So, using the broken binder problem as an example, to be told of this a day before the board meeting is not too bad as there is time to implement a fix. However, to discover half an hour before the meeting that there are no board reports would send most bosses into a mini rage!

The big message… always keep your boss in the loop and avoid giving your boss a nasty shock!

Find the Boss's Hot Buttons:

This may, of course, sound like pandering… but to some degree, so what! If it helps the relationship and you do not feel you are selling your soul then it can be a very smart move to go out of your way to find out what makes your boss purr.

Of course, figuring out just how they like reports formatted is pretty essential, as is getting projects and work done to deadlines. However, taking the time to discover what their interests are, when their birthday is and what football team they support can pay big dividends in the 'getting on' stakes.

Become Uber Reliable:

Becoming a member of your boss's team who they can truly trust and rely on is more valued than you can imagine. So always try to honour commitments, projects and schedules. If you say you will get it done then get it done, and if you can't then let your boss know nice and early. Keep things that need to be confidential confidential – and while it may, at times, be difficult not to 'share' feelings and opinions with colleagues, try not to bad mouth your boss. If they ever hear of it on the grapevine, it will truly not help the relationship.

Never Go Over Your Boss's Head:

Never go behind your boss's back to their boss, unless of course there is a dire need to. Things that fall under the 'Dire Need' heading are:

- Something important that you are working on has a serious problem and it needs **urgent** attention. However, despite you talking to them about it in detail, your boss refuses to face this and they are ignoring it. A catastrophe is looming and they are doing nothing to avoid it.

- Your boss is doing something illegal.

- Your boss has a serious physical or mental illness but is not really accepting this.

- Your boss has a substance abuse problem.

- Your boss is doing something that would fall under gross misconduct (sexual harassment, racism etc.).

Now the above list is, of course, not definitive and there could be other situations that warrant going immediately to a more senior manager. However, these exceptional circumstances apart, take care not to be disloyal by going above their head. It does nothing for the generation of trust and mutual respect.

The Last Thought…

It is possible that you may indeed spend more time in the company of your boss than you do with your loved one. Therefore, doesn't it make sense to be constantly working on and investing in the relationship?

The world is full of employee/boss relationships that, at first, were pretty dire, but then were worked on and transformed into something truly fantastic. Developing a great relationship with your boss can take time and effort – but it's so worth it!